ALECKY BLYTHE

In 2003, Alecky founded Recorded Delivery. The term
'recorded delivery' has now become synonymous with the
particular verbatim technique she employs. Her first play *Come
Out Eli* at the Arcola won the Time Out Award for the Best
Production on the Fringe and transferred to the BAC for the
Critic's Choice Season. Other work for theatre includes *Little
Revolution* at the Almeida; *London Road*, which she co-
authored with composer Adam Cork, won Best Musical at the
Critics' Circle Awards and played at the National Theatre in
2011 (Cottesloe) and 2012 (Olivier); *Do We Look Like
Refugees?!* at the Assembly Rooms, Edinburgh (Fringe First
Award); *Friday Night Sex* at the Royal Court; *Decade* for
Headlong and National Theatre; *The Girlfriend Experience* at
the Royal Court and Drum, Plymouth and Young Vic; *I Only
Came Here for Six Months* for KVS and Halles de Schaerbeeck,
Brussels; *Where Have I Been All My Life?* at the New Vic;
Cruising at the Bush; *Strawberry Fields* for Pentabus and *All
the Right People Come Here* at the New Wimbledon. TV
includes *The Riots; In their Words* (writer and co-director) and
A Man in a Box. Film includes *London Road* (adaptation),
Waiting for God (short film, writer and director).

Alecky Blythe

OUR
GENERATION

NICK HERN BOOKS
London
www.nickhernbooks.co.uk

A Nick Hern Book

Our Generation first published in Great Britain in 2022 as a paperback original by Nick Hern Books Limited, The Glasshouse, 49a Goldhawk Road, London W12 8QP

Our Generation copyright © 2022 Alecky Blythe

Alecky Blythe has asserted her right to be identified as the author of this work

Cover photography by Simon Sorted
Art Direction by National Theatre Graphic Design Studio

Designed and typeset by Nick Hern Books, London
Printed in Great Britain by Mimeo Ltd, Huntingdon, Cambridgeshire PE29 6XX

A CIP catalogue record for this book is available from the British Library

ISBN 978 1 83904 065 8

Our Generation was first performed in the Dorfman auditorium
of the National Theatre, London, on 23 February 2022
(previews from 14 February), before transferring to the Minerva
Theatre, Chichester, on 22 April 2022. The cast was as follows:

YOUNGSTERS

ANNABELLA/EDITH/JEMIMA   Alex Jarrett

ROBYN/ISLA/ALI'S FORM   Anna Burnett
TEACHER/LEENA

AYESHA/LUAN'S ENGLISH   Anushka Chakravarti
TEACHER/KEISHA

TAYLOR/LUAN'S PE   Callum Mardy
TEACHER/AIDEN/

CALLUM/BEN/CAI   Conor Gormally

ZAC/DRIN/LUAN'S SCIENCE   Dee Ahluwalia
TEACHER/EX BOYFRIEND

ALI/IESTYN/ASIF/KEMI/ROB   Gavi Singh Chera

LUAN/GAVIN   Hélder Fernandes

LUCAS/KENDAL   Joe Bolland

EMILY/HELEDD/   Poppy Shepherd
ANNABELLA'S MATHS
TEACHER/CADI

IERUM/JODI

MIA/HEBE/CALLUM'S   Sarita Gabony
ENGLISH TEACHER/JAZZ

ADULTS

ALBERTA/MISS RODRIGUES/   Debbie Chazen
MARTINA/PATRICIA/MIG/JEN/
GRANNY

AGRON/MR WYN HUWS/   Hasan Dixon
SPORTS TEACHER/
AUDIENCE MEMBER/
MR CHAPMAN/GEORGE/
BOYS' BRIGADE CAPTAIN/JAY/
MR DAWSON/UNCLE/BEAUTICIAN/
REVEREND STUART ROBERTSON/
MR SULLIVAN/RONALD/
MR THOMPSON

LULJETA/NAJMA/MUSIC   Stephanie Street
TEACHER/MARGARET/
MISS BRADLEY/TASMIN/
MONNA/MISS NOTLEY

All other parts played by members of the company

Director	Daniel Evans
Set Designer	Vicki Mortimer
Costume Designer	Kinnetia Isidore
Lighting Designer	Zoe Spurr
Movement Director	Carrie-Anne Ingrouille
Music Composition,	D.J. Walde
Production and Direction	
Sound Designer	Paul Arditti
Video Designer	Akhila Krishnan
Dramaturgy	Sebastian Born
Creative Producer	Pádraig Cusack
Casting	Charlotte Sutton CDG
Dialect Coaches	Charmian Hoare and Shereen Ibrahim
Company Voice Work	Jeannette Nelson
Staff Director	Stephen Bailey
Collectors	Alecky Blythe, Izzy Dougill, Leah Gaffey, Dan Murphy, Ruth Tebby and Olivia Wilkes

Introduction
Alecky Blythe

Our Generation was first conceived in 2015 not long after
Rufus Norris was appointed Artistic Director at the National, as
a way of gaining an insight into the generation of young people
in the UK coming of age in the 2020s. Early on I realised that in
order to deliver a play with a scale that could go some way to
representing the geographical breadth of the country, I was
going to need some assistance. I enlisted the help of five
budding verbatim practitioners, not long out of university, who
were eager to develop their skills in the field. As I was already
collecting interviews at a school in South London, five other
schools were found nationally for each of my collector
assistants to visit.

I knew I wanted to present a rich variety of teenagers from a
range of backgrounds and it took a good few visits over the first
six months to locate them. Initially every month the collectors
would send me ninety minutes of their highlights, which over
time I would boil down further. Then once all the subjects had
been chosen and good connections had been formed with them
and their families, we cut the visits back to once every couple of
months.

Who could have imagined what was in store as we headed into
2020? The plan had always been that we would end the
interviewing process that autumn so when the first lockdown
was implemented, thanks to video calls and FaceTime, we were
able to move our in-person interviews to mobiles relatively
seamlessly. It was extraordinary to be documenting these
teenagers for such a long time, expecting – like they were – for
their futures to be moving forward to the next stage of
development when suddenly the world stopped. Of course
Covid has had a major impact on all of our lives, but I think the
disruption it has had on teenagers has been immeasurable.
I hope the play goes some way to expressing not only how they
have suffered but also how impressively they have found hope
and resilience through it.

Over the course of the five years of collecting, I benefitted from
a series of workshops at the NT Studio which were incredibly

helpful in allowing me and the director, Daniel Evans, to explore the material. At one point a workshop was almost derailed by the second lockdown but operations were niftily moved onto Zoom, thanks to our sound engineer Adrien Corcilius. By that stage the collecting period had come to an end so it was the first time that I'd created the full draft and it amounted to a five-hour marathon performance on Zoom. Since then, as I have continued to chip away at the edifice with the brilliant help and expertise of dramaturg Sebastian Born, a more concise structure has emerged which, although still epic, I hope is more palatable for a theatre audience.

As I proofread this final draft of the play, three days away from our first preview, Covid continues to wreak havoc on our industry and threaten the life of the show. One of our actors has tested positive so Leah Gaffey, one of the collectors, who is also an actor and conveniently Welsh (which is the required accent for the part) is currently winging her way from Wales to take up the role. It's a wonderful example of the unstoppable spirit manifest in the excellent team I have been lucky enough to work with.

The commitment of the entire cast and creatives has been breathtaking and a clear illustration of their belief in the importance of portraying these young people's lives authentically on stage. It's due to the leadership of Daniel Evans as director and Pádraig Cusack as creative producer that this level of dedication has been instilled in the company, so inspiring are they to collaborate with. I want to thank them sincerely for their support and dynamism during the show's development, during which there were times I feared we wouldn't make it to the stage at all, such were the challenges.

Ironically I remember sitting in Rufus's office when we first started talking about the project and I told him of my reservations about writing a piece that could be potentially so freewheeling. I wondered how on earth I would structure it without a central event to aid knitting it together. 'You never know what might happen over the next five years,' he said. 'There could be wars, terrorist attacks, a pandemic.' I don't think anyone would wish for what we have all been through over the last couple of years or could have predicted that his words would turn out to be so uncannily prophetic, but I want to thank him for encouraging me to take up the gauntlet.

The Collectors

Glasgow	Izzy Dougill
Belfast	Dan Murphy
Anglesey	Leah Gaffey
Birmingham	Olivia Wilkes
Northamptonshire	Ruth Tebby
South London	Alecky Blythe

Special thanks to the twelve teenagers who generously shared their lives with us, and to their families, friends and teachers who also allowed us in. Quite simply, without them, there would be no play.

In memory of my dear friends
Catherine Nix-Collins and Ben Chatfield

Characters

SOUTH LONDON

IERUM, *North African, twelve**
MASARRAT, *Ierum's brother, North African, seven*
MASOOD, *Ierum's brother, North African, eight*

LUAN, *British, Kosovan, fifteen**
DRIN, *Luan's brother, Kosovan, eighteen*
AGRON, *Luan's father, Kosovan, forties*
LULJETA, *Luan's mother, Kosovan, forties*

BELFAST

ANNABELLA, *dual heritage, thirteen**
ALBERTA, *Annabella's mother, white, forties*

CALLUM, *white, thirteen**
MARGARET, *Callum's mother, white, forties*
RONALD, *Callum's father, white. forties*

CAMBRIDGESHIRE

EMILY, *white, fourteen**
JEN, *Emily's mother, white, forties*

LUCAS, *white, fourteen**

GLASGOW

ZAC, *dual heritage, fifteen**
NAJMA, *Zac's mother, Indian, forties*

ROBYN, *white, fifteen**
MIG, *Robyn's mother, white, fifties*
JAY, *Robyn's father, white, forties*

NORTH WALES

MIA, *white, fourteen**
MARTINA, *Mia's mother, white, forties*

TAYLOR, *white, wheelchair user, fourteen**
PATRICIA, *Taylor's mother, white, forties*
GEORGE, *Taylor's father, white, wheelchair user, forties*
DYLAN, *Taylor's brother, white, eight*
KEG, *Taylor's half-brother, white, nineteen*

BIRMINGHAM

ALI, *Pakistani, fifteen**
AYESHA, *Ali's sister, Pakistani, twelve**
TASMIN, *Ali and Ayesha's mother, Pakistani, forties*

* The ages given here refer to how old the youngsters were at the beginning of the interviewing process.

TEACHERS
MR WYN HUWS
MISS RODRIGUES
MUSIC TEACHER
SPORTS TEACHER
MRS MCAULEY
MR CHAPMAN
MISS BRADLEY
MR DAWSON
CALLUM'S ENGLISH
TEACHER
LUAN'S HISTORY
TEACHER
ALI'S FORM TEACHER
ANNABELLA'S MATHS
TEACHER
LUAN'S ENGLISH
TEACHER
LUAN'S SCIENCE
TEACHER
LUAN'S PE TEACHER
MRS JONES
MISS BURROWS
MONNA
REVEREND STUART
ROBERTSON
MR SULLIVAN
MISS NOTLEY
MR THOMPSON

FRIENDS
MAGGIE
DILYS
CHARISSE
HELEDD
ANWEN
CRAIG
CORNELL
MOHAMMED
JAYDEN
NILES

SHANICE
ISLA
EDITH
HEBE
BEN, *Lucas's best friend*
HANNAH
EVA
JEMIMA
GAVIN, *Mia's boyfriend*
JAKE
FRIEND 1, 2 *and* 3
CASEY
KENDAL
IESTYN
ASIF
LEENA, *Taylor's girlfriend*
SEB
KEMI
KIRSTY
KEISHA
LILY
SIOBHAN
AIDEN
CADI
JODI
MIA'S EX BOYFRIEND
OSCAR
PIP
LUELLA
SASHA
ROB, *Robyn's boyfriend*
JAZ, *Zac's girlfriend*
CAI, *Mia's new boyfriend*

OTHERS
AUDIENCE MEMBER
BOYS' BRIGADE CAPTAIN
COUSIN 1
UNCLE
GRANNY
BEAUTICIAN
COUSIN 2

Note on the Text

A forward slash in the text (/) indicates the point at which the next speaker interrupts.

Inconsistencies in spelling and grammar are deliberate and indicate idiosyncracies in the speech and delivery of the characters.

All names have been changed for safeguarding purposes.

Notes on Performance

During rehearsals the actors worked directly from the audio interviews, listening to them very carefully through earphones and copying the exact speech pattern as they performed. Eventually the earphones have come off and the lines have been learnt but the actors maintain the original delivery, having learnt the lines incredibly precisely savouring every minute vocal detail that can be heard in the audio.

This text went to press before the end of rehearsals and so may differ slightly from the play as performed.

PART ONE

ACT ONE

1.1.1. Hello world

An empty stage. A narrow ramp runs along the back wall from stage-right. There is a hatch in the back wall, upstage-left.

IERUM *enters and stands upstage-centre. She looks around the auditorium in awe.*

IERUM. Hello world.

1.1.2. Opening

Music plays. The other eleven youngsters enter and join IERUM. *As they dance to the music vigorously a projection on the back wall reads, 'Twelve teenagers interviewed over five years, in their own words.' A second projection reads 'Their names have been changed to protect their identities.' The music fades to a low level as* ANNABELLA *starts talking.*

ANNABELLA. God is angry with the terrorism out in the world. I just, I know it and, I really and – I really, I hate to say but I do think that we will be part of the apocalypse.

LUAN. You hear my name everywhere, everyone's just talking about me, everyone's excited (*Claps his hands.*) about me. Yeah my dad, my dad, my dad was so proud I could just see, he was so proud. All my family members were like, 'I put my name, our na– our family name on the map.'

ROBYN. We didn't go away this year. Ah – we just had to – we had to buy a boiler this year (*Laughing.*) so it's either a boiler or a holiday so (*Laughing.*) we got a boiler.

TAYLOR. My dad started crying when he found out I was on the twenty-threes team, 'eah. (*Laughs.*) I was there laughing at him, it's funny. To me it's just a team. Like playing for the local team.

MIA. I've stopped going out, I've got no friends, I've got no life. I've got no friends left.

EMILY. If, I've never, I never go anywhere. I'm quite stressed out at the moment. (*Laughs.*) So I've got Biology block test tomorrow basically on everything we've learnt this year. And I know absolutely nothing.

ZAC. Last week I had, I had, what was it, six concerts in five days? I've been finding it really hard to get into festive spirit cos everyone's like 'you've got all these pre-lims' and not – they're not even important but they're like, they're your first exams so like 'ahhh' and you got all the concerts 'yaahhh'.

CALLUM. Cos I'm not like a, I'm not a fighter it sounds weird cos I wanna be a wrestler but I'm not like a fighter y'know, oh I don't take pain very well.

AYESHA. Celebrities are like a big part of my life because I've always wanted to become one.

ALI. Kim Kardashian got robbed / I feel so sorry for her.

AYESHA *gasps*.

Oh, I need to start revising. I'm actually frightened, of life.

AYESHA. I wanna go Hajj so bad. And Australia I wanna getta tan.

ALI. I want to go to America so bad.

AYESHA. I hate you so / much.

ALI. I hate you more.

LUCAS. Mum, when you're watching this, (*Laughs.*) I-I did have a girlfriend during exams, don't be angry, okay? It was really good for me, m– really helpful. (*Chuckles.*)

1.1.3. Switched

A projection on the back wall reads, 'IERUM, South London.'

IERUM*'s school.*

IERUM. I switched, um, friends groups. Er, I'm hanging more round with Sienna, cos like, Sienna's a quiet girl and she hangs around with, like, people like Amy and Charity and they're, like, quiet people. And then, yeah cos of that, I think that if I continue hanging round with her then I will get myself into less trouble. I just think that it'll be better for me cos when I'm with the other group I tend to get – I tend to find myself in a sticky situation sometimes but when I'm with the group that Sienna's in everyfing's like all calm... yeah. W– like, th-there's nothing exciting that's really going sort f– really exciting, so 'n' it kinda bores me. But I can't go back to the other group, and also I can't be lonely.

Sometimes I doubt myself because of my colour. I – I just don't think I'd fit in. I'm the only black girl who actually tried to attempt this. I'm, I'm, like, trying to copy them so I'm trying to become like them. So what I do, what they usually do, is they sit down and they talk quietly, and they, like, laugh poshly. So then that's what I do too; I sit down, talk quietly an' laugh poshly: 'ha-ha-ha-ha-ha-ha'. Yeah somefing like that!

I just feel like if I get close to Sienna, cos I don't really have my phone she has her phone all the time she's on Instagram and stuff. And I don't really have Instagram and all them apps, um, because my phone isn't, like, an Apple phone, and whatnot. I can't just suddenly tell her that my parents made a rule that I'm only allowed on my phones on Saturdays and Sundays. (*Sighing.*) I don't know, mean like, children these days are pretty different. (*Pause.*) Yeah. W-we're very different. It makes me feel, like, ohh, w-why can't I ever be like them?

1.1.4. Fail at life

A projection on the back wall reads, 'MIA, North Wales.'

Playground at MIA*'s school.*

MAGGIE. Who are we red army?

DILYS. Who are we red army?

MAGGIE. Who are we red army?

MIA. Hi, my name's Mia Parry and it's my birfday in November, can you all get me a present?

MAGGIE. No.

CHARISSE. No! (*Laughs.*)

MIA. And my dad's Aaron Parry!

HELEDD. We're all revising for our important exams / that are coming up in a few…

MIA. Cos we have exams in three weeks. / What?

HELEDD. Weeks. Cos we're in Year 10 and it's an important year. And we have to revise, otherwise we'll get a bad mark and then we won't get a good job.

MIA. Then you'll fail at / life.

HELEDD. And then we'll / just fail at life and you / just have to go on the dole an' stuff. And you don't / wanna do that. You just have to work hard and / be good.

CHARISSE. Yep.

MIA. Oh, I don't mind.

ANWEN. Bell's – bell's gone. Bell's gone!

MIA. Go on.

MAGGIE. But she doesn't do anything.

MIA (*laughs*). / I –

HELEDD. She just fails at life.

MIA. / Yeah.

HELEDD. That's what she wants to do – (*Laughs.*)

MIA. I fail at everyfin'.

HELEDD. Cos you don't try. I'm not shutting up / (*Laughs.*)

MIA. Heledd 'I love you'?

HELEDD. I love you too.

MIA. I know.

MAGGIE (*murmurs*). / A mother.

MIA. I'm –

> *They all sing 'Jeremy Kyle' by Lucy Spraggan.*

MAGGIE. Robbed me there…

MIA. This is my jam.

> I wanna be on *The Jeremy Kyle Show* it looks good. Um, I lost my dad, yeah, can you help me find 'im? (*Laughs.*) If I get caught with my phone I'm dead. Or I'll get it taken off me again. You can't see it but I've got, like, twenty quid in this bra, iPhone 5C in this bra.

MR WYN HUWS. Mia? Ga'i air.

MIA. Hi, sir.

MR WYN HUWS. Iawn? Ga'i air efo chdi plis?

MIA. What have I done wrong?

1.1.5. New Spanish teacher

A projection on the back wall reads, 'LUAN, South London.'

LUAN*'s Spanish lesson.*

MISS RODRIGUES. Er, alright!

> / Er, I haven't met most of you, I'm the new Spanish teacher, my name is Miss Rodrigues.

CRAIG. Ohh Spanish, my gaad.

CORNELL. Thank you!

CRAIG. Another one.

MOHAMMED. Another one.

CRAIG. / Another one.

JAYDEN. Another one.

CORNELL. Thank you!

NILES. Another one.

MISS RODRIGUES. And…?

LUAN. Our teacher's been gone forever. She left one day and never came back. (*Whispers.*) I don't think she'll last. (*Loudly.*) Aiite sorry to disturb the class, who has my book?

CRAIG. Where's my book?

MISS RODRIGUES. Well, if it's not over there, look, look over there, there are a million folders.

CRAIG. M– Moha– Mohammed, go on i– BBC tonight at six-thirty, you'll see me, / you'll see me. Luan, innit if you go on BBC One tonight.

MISS RODRIGUES. Er, Shazia? Er Niles?

NILES. Yeeess.

LUAN. Yeah, we're on BBC One today, for basketball. So um, / we're we're in LeBron James / Academy, so, it's an academy wh– er NBA player is like –

CRAIG. BBC One, Cornell?

MISS RODRIGUES. Er, Paula.

Er, Luan?

LUAN. Came to our –

MISS RODRIGUES. Hola?

LUAN. Hola, / me llamo – sorry?

MISS RODRIGUES. Did you find your book? / Did you find –

LUAN. Sorry? / No I did not.

MISS RODRIGUES. Your book? Well then look for it.

LUAN. Er, I'll do that after. Er, well, er NBA player sponsors our academy basically, it's / it's in the sports hall down there.

SHANICE. Lu-an! Your folder was here.

LUAN. Do I care? / Sorry about that, interrupted rudely, um.

MOHAMMED (*laughs*). He's, he's like one of the best in Lambeth.

LUAN. Thanks man. Say that again.

MOHAMMED (*very loudly*). He's one of the best / in Lambeth!

LUAN (*laughs*). But yeah I wanna make this my career / cos right now school's not doing well. (*Sniffs twice.*) And also I wanna be, I wanna be that guy who makes it out the 'hood.

CORNELL *barks*.

MISS RODRIGUES. De nada.

MOHAMMED *laughs*.

LUAN. Why you laughin'?

CRAIG. I find trappin' dead man.

LUAN (*laughs*). Miss any more? (*Beat.*) The GCSEs are coming up, so we have to put our heads down, it's not really that hard. I say, yeah, all you need to do is revise on the last c-couple o' weeks and you'll get good grades. All I'm thinking to do right now is go high school, division-one high school named Blair Academy, it's in America. My mum and dad they don't want me to go. I'm their little baby and stuff like that but I'm going. Have you guys got the map in your planners? / Wait, let me get, let me get my planner.

MOHAMMED. Map, yeah. (*Beat.*) He's travelled like bare places ennit?

MOHAMMED *passes his planner to* LUAN.

CRAIG. Are you showing her where Kosco is?

LUAN (*referring to the map in the planner*). Yep. So an' obviously yeah, you see Serbia, very er, er, I'm gonna give you a history lesson, so obviously there was a big war in

Yugoslavia, and Serbia had a big war with Kosovo, so then they started attacking them, so my mum and dad ran away and they went to England, and then, that's where we are now.

1.1.6. I'll be on TV

A projection on the back wall reads, 'TAYLOR, North Wales.'

TAYLOR*'s school.*

TAYLOR. Yesterday we won the, erm, North Wales league, undefeated team. It's only – I'm only excited cos I'll be on TV. My dad started crying when he found out I was on the twenty-threes team, 'eah. (*Laughs.*) I was there laughing at him, it's funny. To me it's just a team. Like playing for the local team. My dad plays with me too, an' my little brother. My dad used to play running basketball for Wales, when he was my age but then he got into a chair and now he's just play basket– wheelchair basketball. An' then I'm basically doing what my dad wanted to do, that's why I'm doing it so. (*Beat.*) But now – (*Beat.*) I'm representing my country – (*Beat.*) so that's alright. I'm just a normal kid. Jus' a normal geezer.

1.1.7. Goat on Chapel Lawn

A projection on the back wall reads, 'EMILY, Cambridgeshire.'

A dormitory at EMILY*'s school.*

EMILY. Oh! Whoever like sponsored the like, paid for the Bristol Gallery blah blah blah like his son was like Head Boy or something and apparently he like made up this rule with it, like um –

ISLA. If Head, Head Girl and Head Boy get married they get to live there.

EMILY. Yeah. / Is that true?

ISLA. Yeah and oh Head Boy's allowed to keep a goat on Chapel Lawns. (*Beat.*)

EMILY. I'd keep a goat on Chapel Lawns.

EDITH. I would.

HEBE. I wanna be a / boy.

ISLA. Shame we're a girl. Dammit.

EDITH. No, but I swear any Head of School –

EMILY. No, Edith, become Head Girl, sta– start your run for
Head Girl now. (*Laughing.*) Pippa, Pippa / FP's starting her
run for Head of House it's really funny. She was telling us all
about it.

Beat.

EDITH. No but…

Are we staying up tonight?

ISLA. Yes, we are.

HEBE. / No.

EDITH. Last night we were meant to stay up –

HEBE. – No cos it's Sunday night.

EMILY. I'm gonna go at like o'clock-ish.

EDITH. You do that, you-you / do that Emily.

HEBE. There's no such thing as o'clock-ish.

ISLA. The funny thing is Emily, we don't care… / cos you're in
Upton!

EDITH. Yeah.

EMILY *laughs*.

And we don't want you.

EMILY. This is Upton, which is the day house. I'm in the day
house because my dad works in the school, he's a
housemaster, I just happen to live with one of the boys'
boarding houses. Boarders are just like, they don't dislike us,
but they're just like 'ew Uptoners' well they do like us, but
then they still tease us about it. Umm, so at the moment this
– these are the two cricket fields cos basically in the summer
term there's so many options for sport. Cos there's

swimming for boys and girls, rowing for boys and girls, then there's athletics for boys and girls, tennis for boys and girls, and then cricket for just boys and rounders for just girls, so there's literally in the summer I – it's crazy how many sports options there are, so at the moment these are two cricket matches, Elland against... I have no idea – (*Laughs*.)

1.1.8. Kyeshadow

A projection on the back wall reads, 'AYESHA, Birmingham.'

AYESHA's *school.*

AYESHA. I'm getting a lot of detentions recently, ta, innit, but I got like two Chanel bags sitting at home and three Versace bags at home and then designer shoes. Y'know Kylie Jenner miss? I've got her lip kit at home. Innit. I'm on that target for getting Kyeshadow. I'm looking for Kylie's, um, Valentime's kit to come out, hopefully I'll be the first person to get it. Ah. Celebrities are like a big part of my life because I've always wanted to become one. And then I've also always wanted to become a dancer. And my dad's like 'oh, don't do something with your life that you're gonna earn money for nothing'. He's like 'oh become a teacher or a doctor or something like that, and I'm 'no doctor'. Don't – I don't even know do science! Oo, science is so hard!

1.1.9. Girlfriend

A projection on the back wall reads, 'LUCAS, Cambridgeshire.'

LUCAS's *common room.*

LUCAS. Looking forward to the new year. It's gunna be good, it's gunna be interest-intense because it's the start of our GCSE course.

BEN. Mm. / Bit nervous.

LUCAS. Yeah kind of. I'm just looking forward to meeting the third / form.

BEN. Third, yeah. I wanna see what they're like, see if they're nice.

LUCAS. Yeah. Some of them are really nice. You know Casper / Willoughby-York?

BEN. Yeah.

LUCAS. Yeah. I beat him at tennis at Framlingham. / Get my point across.

BEN. Is he-is he nice?

LUCAS. His sister's called Itka.

New third-formers walk past the window.

BEN. Is that them?

LUCAS *looks out the window.*

LUCAS. Yes. Woh they're so small! We're gunna be really nice to / them.

BEN. Yeah.

Support them.

LUCAS. Yeah.

BEN. Yeah.

LUCAS. And James, he's on his gap year now, he got into Cambridge, so…

BEN. I like Cambridge.

LUCAS. Yeah, Cambridge is / nice.

BEN. Yeah. Do you wanna go to Cambridge?

LUCAS. No, not really. / My dad went to Durham, I'd like to go to Durham. / Never know, fingers crossed hopefully / hopefully get a girlfriend. (*Laughs.*)

BEN. No.

Yeah.

(*Laughs.*) Yeah.

Maybe you'll, maybe you'll bring your girlfriend sitting here instead of me.

LUCAS. Yeah. In two months' time, in two months' time.

BEN. Yeah. That's, that's, at – / yeah, make, yeah that's your aim.

LUCAS. That's my aim, that's my aim, make that my aim, for Ben not to be sitting here / in two. (*Laughs*.)

BEN. Yeah. That'd be a bit awkward.

LUCAS. Yeah that'd be really / funny.

BEN. Yeah. Yeah, what would you talk about?

LUCAS (*laughs*). Ru – like… oh we've got the club as well!

BEN. Oh, yeah.

LUCAS. And you can invite third-formers to come in / then –

BEN. Can you? So if you had a girlfriend and / in third form then you could just invite her in?

LUCAS. Exactly. Ohh, although she has to go ho– back early.

BEN. Mm, that's true.

LUCAS. Yeah. I'll sacrifice my partying for her / cos I'm such a charming.

BEN (*laughs*). It's only like fifteen minutes, later isn't / it's so useless.

LUCAS. Yeah I know, pretty useless.

And I've got *Les Mis*. / That'll be fun.

BEN. Oh yeah.

LUCAS. I'm like 'Sailor Number Four – '

BEN *laughs*.

(*Laughs*.) I'd love to be an actor but I think that'll, there's, I've just gotta –

BEN. You meet loads of cool people.

LUCAS. And you get a hu / ton o' money – (*Laughs*.)

BEN. Like Jennifer Aniston and like –

LUCAS. I don't think Sailor Four will be doing very well.

BEN. No.

LUCAS (*laughs*). And we should go down to the river, / when it's summer.

BEN. Yeah.

Mmhm.

LUCAS. With our girlfriends.

BEN. Yeah.

LUCAS. Yeah. Yeah – (*Chuckles.*) / Love that.

BEN *chuckles*.

LUCAS *chuckles*.

BEN. Yeah.

1.1.10. I love my religion

A projection on the back wall reads, 'ALI, Age 14, Birmingham.'

ALI*'s music lesson.*

ALI. My mum is from here and my dad's from Pakistan. I'm going into Year 11 like next year so, oh my god miss I'm so scared. Miss, because my GCSEs are like coming up and it – I'm just scared if like I fail or something. In reality I wanna become a lawyer – (*Laughs.*) a criminal one. And then my dreams are just I wanna become famous.

MUSIC TEACHER. Today's focus is to do task one. I would like everybody to have had a go at finishing task one maybe working on to task two.

ALI. Okay.

MUSIC TEACHER. Are you doing a protest song or a changing of the season song? / Er wait a second, I'm listening to Jimmy for a bit.

ALI. What shall I put – protesting against what? Not mixing culture with religion because our religion is mixed with culture a lot. Killing is prohibited in our religion and you see

ISIS people killing. And obviously that is my religion and we have like, I dunno how to say, our God, we have to worship him and we read the Qur'an and then like obviously it's really, really good and I like I love my religion and do you know like we have to pray five times a day but I'll be honest miss I don't sometimes. It's just, I don't do it and then I feel bad afterwards. So, I'm gonna start, miss, praying again.

1.1.11. Apocalypse

A projection on the back wall reads, 'ANNABELLA, Belfast.'

ANNABELLA*'s school canteen.*

ANNABELLA. My friend and I tried to summon Satan to my friend's house. We tried to make a Ouija board and then –

HANNAH . Oh wh– why would / you do that?

ANNABELLA. Cos, I don't know.

I really and – I really, I hate to say but I do think that we will be part of the apocalypse. And what scares me most, I don't really go to church but I do read the Bible and scares me that I don't go to church, right? And God said that anyone there, erm, people who do go to church like Hannah and stuff, will be lifted straight up to God and go to Heaven, but we – the people that, there's tons of pe–, there's probably tons of people in the school that don't even go to church or whatever you know? – and we will be sent up to God and we will be judged and finally we'll go to Hell. That's something that I really worry about. (*Beat.*) I don't like school. / No –

EVA. We hate school.

The hatch opens to reveal the DINNER LADY *dishing out pizzas.*

HANNAH. Pizza!

EVA. Yeah, we got pizza.

ANNABELLA. The pizzas went up by twenty pee a slice. Eva likes to think that she's queen.

EVA. I am the queen!

ANNABELLA. You're not. / You're not. I've been queen since, like, before all of you. I've always been queen.

EVA. Yes I am!

ANNABELLA. I'm an only child. It's me, my mum, my cat, my dog and my deceased chicken.

1.1.12. Discipline

A projection on the back wall reads, 'ZAC, Glasgow.'

ZAC*'s home.*

ZAC. Last week I had, I had, what was it, six concerts in five days?

NAJMA. Yeah. Cos it's Christmas isn't it.

ZAC. So I-I get home from a concert at like eleven o'clock and be like working really uggh, and I'd wake up like half-eight the next morning and be like half an hour late to school an'.

NAJMA. It – this is, this is the particularly / er busy time of year.

ZAC. Urgh. I'd practise for like twenty minutes, practise the piano, twenty minutes every single morning. Why? / (*Laughs.*)

NAJMA. Discipline.

ZAC. But c– but I'm like obviously like as I grew up I'd be like why am I doing this? And now, like I, sort of, I'll, I can't, obviously I can't, obviously I can't wake up in the morning now cos I'm like eeeurgh.

NAJMA. We're very strict with them.

ZAC. I didn't even think you were that strict until, like, I'd be at other people's houses. / It was so strict. (*Laughs.*)

NAJMA. But I think you say it-it's the discipline and because, er, we both are involved in music, that's what we do, that's our thing, and you have to be disciplined. He's predicted, his predictions are he's got to / keep to his predictions.

ZAC. By – by my teachers.

NAJMA. His predictions are eight As.

1.1.13. Bullied

A projection on the back wall reads, 'CALLUM, Belfast.'

CALLUM*'s PE lesson.*

SPORTS TEACHER (*shouts*). Right guys, quickly, on the line facing me, c'mon let's go. Now, we're going to do two laps of the pitch today. Now, if you go inside the white line, you're gunna get another lap.

The class follow the teacher's instructions, apart from CALLUM *who stays back to talk.*

CALLUM. I, I don't love football, I, I ruined it for my team (*Laughs.*) well um, I, I suppose because um, ah, whenever we were about to score, I didn't realise it was a free kick right at the net, erm, er, and erm, whenever it got passed I jumped in the way (*Laughs.*) so then the whole team hated me for that. (*Laughs.*) I really, I don't take it under my notice. And then, oh, whenever I went back in the boys were like, 'oh, you gunna go read your book now Cal' – you know trying to make fun of me cos I read books – I'm just like, 'well i-it, it's', I'm like 'yes I am'.

Yeah, well I had to, I had to kinda learn to deal with that, er, in primary school you know cos I was, I was bullied quite a lot in primary school so I had to kinda adapt. Cos I'm not like a, I'm not a fighter it sounds weird cos I wanna be a wrestler but I'm not like a fighter y'know, if someone said some-something to me, you know I just go out and hit them – not that kind of person, er so, I just, I, I decided actually you know what I'm quite good at using my words so – might as well do that.

1.1.14. I'm very left-wing

A projection on the back wall reads, 'ROBYN, Glasgow.'

ROBYN*'s school.*

ROBYN. I'm very left-wing. (*Laughs.*) Cos my mum's from a working-class background and my dad is quite as well but like they're both very left and so is like, cos, M-Mum's a like, all her family are immigrants, and Dad's are Italian travellers so he's like an immigrant as well so they kind of like, it's like, it yeah. They-they will not buy brand Jaffa Cakes cos they're too expensive. Cos like my dad's in temp jobs more than like proper jobs. He like jumps about he d– he's currently in an admin job but sometime, like before that he was working in a call centre on the phones. He's in his forties. My mum's in her fifties though and she's a freelance actress so, like she does um, tourist shows. She used to have to dress up as a massive midgey. (*Beat.*) Uhuh it's like a, it's like a kinda shit mosquito. (*Laughs.*) Um… and they do this whole thing with a haggis and it's like b– (*Laughs.*) It's exactly what you expect from a Scottish tourist show. Like it gets to the point when you've seen your mum like pretend to be a heartbroken lesbian gang member. Like nothing fazes me any more.

1.1.15. Bop Till You Drop

Community centre.

MRS MCAULEY (*shouts*). Good afternoon everyone!

ALL. Good afternoon!

MRS MCAULEY. Good, good, we're awake this afternoon, this is good. Welcome to our Bop Till You Drop annual Christmas show.

ANNABELLA *hugs* ALBERTA *goodbye before going to join the dance troupe gathered upstage.*

ALBERTA. She's so good Annabella, she's such a good child. No bother, no. Very little backchat, nothing, er the next couple of years'll be hard taking her through the whole womanhood thing, you know? But we'll get there. It's such a good turnout, I actually didn't expect it / to be so busy.

AUDIENCE MEMBER. Well last year was good, but this is even better.

ALBERTA. Yeah. This is my first year, you see, because, um, my daughter only joined the hip-hop team, er, I think it was a couple of months just ago, just not long.

AUDIENCE MEMBER. You know what, they're doing very, very well.

ALBERTA. Yeah. The– they diagnosed me wi' arthritis just in my pelvis and it's down my legs, y'know, it affects my legs, an' –

AUDIENCE MEMBER. Well I'm in for two new knees and a hip.

ALBERTA. Uhuh.

ANNABELLA *heads the dance troupe who get into position downstage. 'Pressure' by Chase & Status plays, lights flash. They perform a hip-hop routine which features a solo by* ANNABELLA.

AUDIENCE *cheers and claps.*

/ (*Claps.*) Woooo. Woooo.

The dance ends and the children exit.

Brilliant, wasn't it? And she didn't forget any steps. I really want her to go on the skiing trip but I don't think it'll happen. They're asking too much money for it. One thousand, twenty pounds for four nights. I want her to go and get the most opportunity in life that she can. But it's hard with just me, you know? We've just moved to the new house and I wanna fix it up and stuff.

Yes, Annabella mentioned about doing something special for her thirteenth birthday, which is February; I just can't afford to.

ANNABELLA *enters and joins* ALBERTA.

It's good, you were brilliant.

ANNABELLA. I was really like / nervous coming off, I was
nervous coming off. And when I went on I was okay / and I
was kind of freakin' out in all but an' cos I didn't know, / like
I didn't know.

ALBERTA. Nervous, we knew you were, yeah.

You were brilliant.

Did you get anything off Santa, no?

ANNABELLA. No, cos Santa freaks me out. He could be
anyone with a bomb under his beard.

1.1.16. 'I Got Plenty o' Nuttin'

LUCAS*'s singing lesson.*

MR CHAPMAN *plays the piano accompaniment.*

LUCAS *sings 'I Got Plenty o' Nuttin' from* Porgy and Bess *by
George Gershwin.*

MR CHAPMAN (*stops playing*). Okay, right at the start, start
off it says '*piano leggero*' which means 'lightly'.

LUCAS. Oh, right.

MR CHAPMAN *laughs.*

/ LUCAS *laughs.*

MR CHAPMAN. Okay, so you're a bit, a bit heavy, / sa– save
the big guns till the end, okay? So you're just warming to
your theme at the moment about how it's good to be poor / it,
it, it doesn't make any sense to be rich and wealthy / cos you
can't take it with us. Okay? So you're dum duh da dum duh
da dum duh da ah ah ah ah. (*Starts playing from the start of
the piece.*)

LUCAS. Yeah.

Yep.

Yep.

LUCAS *starts singing again.*

MR CHAPMAN. Off.

LUCAS *continues to sing but can't quite hit the final note.*

Okay that's the bit / that always catches you out isn't it, okay?

LUCAS. Yeah.

1.1.17. The chickens hate me

EMILY*'s home.*

EMILY. So that's like our yard, which is where we keep our chickens and like – We have five chickens. The chickens just hate me so much like, they kind of got bored of being in a coop, cos like obviously all the grass is gone and my mum hated them being around here so they're like, they ate all the plants so, basically she'd open our side gate, and she'd she'd walk through to the front garden, they'd like all follow her in a line and like they listen to her and like they – like whenever she comes they like all follow her and like she gives them food and then one time she went away for a week and I was left in charge of them. And like I'd open the gate and they just wouldn't follow me, they'd just run around, they'd just eat all the plants, they just like hate me so I like, they just don't listen to me, they just don't like me.

1.1.18. Daddy's dream

LUAN*'s home. The table is fully laid, complete with a tablecloth and a seafood pasta dish.*

AGRON. This is an Italian dish that I, I master at. (*Chuckles.*) Traditional dish is her.

LULJETA. Like Balkan foods.

AGRON. Lots of grease in other words.

DRIN. Dig in.

Everyone starts to eat.

LUAN. Broke up, um, on Friday. I go back on Monday. Pretty much just been playing basketball.

LULJETA. They follow Daddy's dream not my dream. Sport, sport, sport, / sport.

AGRON. Daddy's dream? Why Daddy's / dream?

LULJETA. Yeah because you like sport, / you wanted your kids to be –

AGRON. Yeah.

DRIN. Footballers.

LULJETA. Yeah.

LUAN *laughs*.

AGRON (*points to* LUAN). He's born here – (*Points to* DRIN.) he came six month old.

LULJETA. Basic English we knew already.

AGRON. In Yugoslavia then they all, um, teach us in school, you know, as a foreign language was, um, English, so we were lucky in a way, you know? But then again I'm bilinguish so I speak Italian, German. They try to learn Spanish they can't even learn that! It's amazing!

LUAN (*laughs*). Ah well my Spanish class is going very (*Laughs.*) well. / (*Laughs.*)

AGRON. Is it? In his head it's like all about basketball and then he lapsin' on his lessons / that's no good.

LUAN *gasps*.

LUAN. I did my PE GCSE and / I think I got an A.

LULJETA (*offering the audience*). D'y'wanna drink?

AGRON. But you're so athletic, I would expect you to do PE. Do it Maths and / Biology but when we got it, it was all red dots everywhere.

LUAN. Yeah but I r–, I can't do that, I can't –

AGRON. He has to improve it because / if he don't get his A levels or GCSEs, / think of it he's be a basketball, you know?

DRIN. But you can't just do it like (*Clicks fingers.*) that.

He will thoughhh –

LUAN. I will.

LULJETA. But his dream is to become basketball player, I hope one day his dream come true.

AGRON. What would you say if he goes to / America?

LULJETA. I said –

AGRON. For us it's good it takes us out of council flat / (*Laughs*.)

LUAN *laughs*.

DRIN. / Hma.

AGRON. Isn't it Mum?

LULJETA. Yeah.

AGRON. / No, you wouldn't support it?

LULJETA. / No, no, because –

DRIN. Seriously?

LULJETA. Of course, yeah.

AGRON. Would you cry?

LULJETA. No.

LUAN. Would you come with me?

LULJETA. No. America it's too far, I don't like to go and live in America, I'm sorry, Luan.

AGRON. If, if Trump becomes, I think he said he will let special cases in, like your politicians and, er, people that live there he, he's not gonna chuck them / out.

LULJETA. But, w–, no but why would you go in that crazy country if he restrict people who to go and hun / w-who not to go.

DRIN. Yeah it be kinda weird.

LUAN. That's where you wanna play, that's / where – /

AGRON. That's where you wanna be.

LULJETA. Yeah but you / it's –

LUAN. That's / the best.

DRIN. That's what you train for.

LUAN. O' the best, yeah. I'm going America, I'm gonna get a scholarship. Trump's a wasteman. Y'know – y'know – y'know – what if he messes up the NBA?

AGRON. Hey – you make sure here you get fit in. No worry about America or you know.

LUAN *yawns*.

He's, he's already – think of is, i' for here it's all done. So far off. What's the future bringing, you know?

1.1.19. Worries

CALLUM*'s home*.

CALLUM. I can't even begin to imagine what it'll be like in the next ten / years.

MARGARET. Only time will tell, honey.

CALLUM. You know, it's gunna be a lot o' things happening. / Yeah.

MARGARET. He, he just, he worries too much. And sometimes I have to reign him in, say 'Callum listen en– enough, you know, put the studying away, put the pen down, you know, go on your PlayStation for a while', it's like a mother telling her child to go on a PlayStation! / You know? Usually it's gettin' – them off the PlayStation!

CALLUM. Yeah, I know that's not natural.

MARGARET. But as long as you do your best that's all we ask, it's not, it's not as if it – there's a career hinging on these exams or, you know, a – ah, a university place or something, you're twelve!

1.1.20. Released

MIA*'s home.*

MARTINA. I've got no GCSEs. None.

MIA. What?

MARTINA. I haven't got any.

MIA. I thought you had, like, six?

MARTINA. No, none. I didn't like school, didn't do my GCSEs / left home with no results. / Yeah, I left school when I was fifteen.

MIA. You left school early, yeah?

So can I / leave?

MARTINA. So.

No.

MIA. Secretly?

MARTINA. No. But, things are quite up and down aren't they, dear?

MIA. Aren't they getting better, though?

MARTINA. Mm, they're very up and down.

MIA. I got arrested for breaking the house windows. (*Beat.*) Aren't they getting up at the minute, though? I got back in contact with my dad two weeks ago, Wednesday – (*Pause.*) and he's coming back in eight weeks so I'm gunna go stay wi' him for a bit cos it's been a while.

MARTINA. Her dad's in prison at the moment. Well the prison got into contact with him and told him some of the problems that we're having with Mia and he's said that he will keep in contact with her now so I hope that he does because (*Pause.*) it's important isn't it. Mia's hell-bent on having contact an' doing whatever so (*Sniffs.*) there's only so much I can protect her an' look out for her.

MIA. He's being released in eight… so it's either the 1st or the 8th of March.

MARTINA. When he's in his right mind he's a very good dad
but he's very into things that he shouldn't be. Little bit –

MIA. Easy influenced.

MARTINA. Yeah, / he's…

MIA. You can't say he's not?

Pause.

MARTINA. Worries me because her dad's chosen to have a bad
life and I think Mia wants to choose to have the same thing.

MIA. She has Mr Wyn Huws on speed dial.

MARTINA. Yesss.

MIA *laughs.*

I have explained to Mia that the choices that she makes now,
at her age, that's what's gonna affect the rest of her life,
because i' she leaves school with no GCSEs, there's not
much of a future / and you should give –

MIA You left school with no GCSEs!

MARTINA. Okay yeah, I did. O-okay, that's fine, fair point.

1.1.21. Table

ZAC*'s home.*

NAJMA (*chuckling*). H'I said – I said, 'how we, how can we
help you study' and he said 'well actually if we could have a
table by the window in the living room' – it's a bay window –
he goes, 'if we have a table there, I could work there, then I
won't be tempted to lie on my bed.' So I go 'okay!' I borrowed
a little collapsible table, came back in half an hour and I said,
'there's your table'. So he's been sitting at the table. Not
chained, but every day, though he knows he's got assignment
for this assignment for – it's continua' – assessment so he
can't just wait till the – May. He has to do things now. (*To*
ZAC.) S'I was telling them about your assignment for
tomorrow Modern Studies. You've got to do it.

ZAC. Well. I don't have to.

NAJMA. W' do you mean you don't have to?

ZAC. If I don't go into school. (*Beat. Laughs.*) I'm kidding.
Um, but I'd say it's the least important out of all of my
assignments so.

NAJMA. You still have to do it.

ZAC. Yeah.

Silence.

1.1.22. Revision cards

LUCAS. Cos our mocks are coming up. Yeah, erm, so that's
quite nerve-racking. So over half-term I did like all my
revision cards, so I've got them all, and now I just need to
learn them. (*Beat.*) Slightly nervous for GCSEs. I'm sure I'm
gonna do fine it's just like ju' compared with the brothers.
Compared with the rest of the country I'm gonna do great.
I'm pretty-pretty sure of that.

1.1.23. Big boss man

TAYLOR*'s home.*

GEORGE. Ah we're both very proud of you, all of us. Yeah?
You're the first kid in school, with a disability to do erm, /
GSCE –

PATRICIA. GCSEs.

TAYLOR. Gym yeah.

GEORGE. – Gym.

PATRICIA. Yeah I know.

GEORGE. You are a role model yeah?

PATRICIA. You wanna get on the GB squad at least once, as a /
taster yeah.

TAYLOR. Yeah. (*Beat.*) See what happens.

GEORGE. He definitely wants it cos he wants a GB kit.

TAYLOR. I'll only get it for free clothes.

GEORGE *and* PATRICIA *laugh*.

(*Looking at the TV*.) What is it?

PATRICIA. He's get – that's it now. He is the –

TRUMP (*on TV*). We are grateful to President Obama.

PATRICIA. – President. Me being a hairdresser now would love
to take away that bulk behind his ears. It's jus' – horrendous.

DYLAN. Is that Donald Trump?

PATRICIA. Yes it is.

DYLAN. Is the world gonna end?

GEORGE. Oh my god!

PATRICIA. Noooo!

DYLAN. No cos it says on Facebook –

PATRICIA. Noo!

GEORGE. Nooooo.

PATRICIA. It just means that, it just means that they've had a
new boss that's all. They've had a new boss or a headmaster.

PATRICIA. / You have to give him chance.

DYLAN. Is he gonna rule the world?

PATRICIA. He own – he runs America now doesn't he, he's
their big boss man.

DYLAN. We're not going there next year again then.

PATRICIA. No we're not.

Laughter.

We're going to Spain.

DYLAN. Yeah. (*Beat*.) Benidorm.

1.1.24. God bless America

ALI *and* AYESHA*'s home.*

ALI. Kim Kardashian got robbed, I feel so sorry for her. Oh, I need to start revising. I have mocks in erm… May. So I have to revise. So I just don't wanna get a crappy grade. I've only got a month, oh my god. (*Gasps.*) And then my GCSEs are next year. I'm actually frightened, of life. I wish I could start in Year 7 again.

AYESHA. There's like a two-minute chance over the day when we talk. Becos he's always on his phone.

ALI. Oh my god, miss, did you watch *EastEnders* special, it's the New Year's one? / *EastEnders.*

AYESHA. Oh gosh! I can't und'stand it. I hate it so much. It's so boring, like one – / the pub.

ALI. I watch *EastEnders*, every single episode from 2009.

AYESHA. It's so boring and confusing.

ALI. Er, Ramadan starts in the end of May. It's basically we, we / er like –

AYESHA. Let me talk.

ALI. Shut up. From – (*Laughs.*)

AYESHA (*laughs*). He / doesn't go mosque. I go mosque, innit. And it is fun because there're not that many students and the Baji ain't strict, like the mosque teacher, she's really fun. Innit. And, then – I wanna go Hajj so bad. And Australia I wanna getta tan.

ALI. Sh– I don't go mosque, if –

I want to go to America go bad. Oh my god did you watch the in– inauguration? Wow. America got what they deserved, if they wanted Trump as a president then they got him. So.

AYESHA. Me and him, we hate him the most he's just so eurghh / yeah.

ALI. Theresa May's gonna meet with him on Friday. And I hope she just (*Inhales.*) says that 'don't ban Muslims' (*Laughs.*) especially me. / I know!

AYESHA (*laughs*). Your laugh is so annoying.

ALI. You're so (*Laughing*.) dead, Ayesha.

AYESHA (*laughing*). You're so dead too.

ALI (*laughing*). Your conversation is –

AYESHA (*laughing*). Your eyyy, his face is.

AYESHA. I hate you so / much.

ALI. I hate you more. So I think I'll faint if I got to America cos I'll be so happy. I'll probably become famous there. America, god bless America.

AYESHA. Sing the American anthem for them, he's been learning it.

Pause.

ALI. Can't sing, okay? / I can't.

AYESHA (*sings*). Oh say can you see by the / duh early light / who gave us bright something something stars! / (*Laughs*.)

ALI. What a brag. (*Laughs*.) So cringey!

AYESHA (*sings*). The home of the brave. (*Speaks*.) See? (*Laughs*.)

ALI (*laughs*). I'm gonna cringe. I've never d– Give me some chocolate.

1.1.25. Shook my world

ROBYN. D'you know what, this freaked me out and no one's really taking me seriously about it but you know Kim and Kanye's kid / y'know the first one, it's four years old.

JEMIMA. Yeah.

(Beat.) No.

ROBYN. Yeah. No. Like everyone else has been like oh I don't care about Kim an' – Ka' and nor do I, but like / that –

JEMIMA. Yeah, I don't either.

ROBYN. I remember when that kid was born.

JEMIMA. Same here.

ROBYN. I was twelve. Er-it feels like it happened like two years ago / max.

JEMIMA. Oh that's so / weird.

ROBYN. Yeah. / So confusing.

JEMIMA. I thought she was like two.

ROBYN. Yeah. No, I thought she was like a proper little toddler but she's / like almost a child.

JEMIMA. Ooops. (*Laughs.*)

Damn.

ROBYN. That's like shook my world.

1.1.26. Met on Snapchat

MIA*'s trailer at home.*

GAVIN *is looking at his phone.*

MIA *shows off her Disney phone cover.*

MIA. It's cute, yeah? I love Disney. But I'm not allowed to watch any of the films.

GAVIN. Not with me anyway. Cos they're / shit.

MIA. I love it. I wanna go to Disneyland.

GAVIN *takes photo of* MIA.

You're a cunt.

GAVIN. N'aw, sly.

GAVIN *takes another photo of* MIA.

MIA. Sto-o-o-op! You know I haven't brushed my hair for like two days!

GAVIN (*chuckles*). I'm Gavin and I'm Mia's boyfriend.

MIA. Just some prick that I found. That's the nicest thing I can say about you today, sorry babes.

GAVIN *takes another photo of* MIA.

Prick. Me and Gavin met on Snapchat, which was a big waste of time. Shoulda deactivated my account. (*Pause*.) Like I used to use my Snapchat all the time, I used to message like loads of different people but I just don't message anyone any more. Cos-like I used to be able to wake up to like a hundred and twenty messages. Now I only wake up to like fifty.

GAVIN *takes another photo of* MIA.

I haven't got all day to sit there like that.

GAVIN *starts to roll a cigarette*.

Like, I got nine'een likes on that, eighty-two on that, hundred and twenty on that, a hundred and three on that, a hundred and twenty-two on that. Make me one.

GAVIN. No.

MIA. Make me one!

GAVIN. / Nnnnnno.

MIA (*inhales*). Make, eurgh fuck, ohh, please! Please! Oh my goduh. It's my fucking bacco he was using the fucking skint prick. You gotta make me a fag please. Well I can't roll with, like, my nails on, yeah, cos my nails, like, longer than my future. So – no / they are though.

GAVIN. What future?

(*Scoffs*.) I said what future.

MIA. I have a future, it's a lot bigger than yours.

GAVIN. Doesn't count though, cos I've got a-a – I'm, like.

MIA. At least I'm gunna leave school with a GCSE.

GAVIN. I have a GCSEs anyway.

MIA. No you haven't, / you haven't got any.

GAVIN. Yes, I do.

MIA. You sat there the other night; 'I haven't got any GCSEs, it's alright, you don't need them'.

GAVIN. You don't need them. (*Coughs*.)

MIA. I just dunno, I jus' – don't think. I dunno… I'm still thinking of going in the army, yeah, but my mam won't let me. (*Pause*.) Why are you such a knob? I actually hate you, you know sometimes. I can't wait for you to leave.

GAVIN. Then I will.

MIA. Oh my god.

GAVIN (*laughs*). Do you want me to come back?

MIA. If you want to.

GAVIN. Well then yeah I will.

MIA. Okay sound.

1.1.27. Funsense

IERUM*'s home*.

IERUM. To be honest with you before I went secondary school I thought that the kids they wou' be like really mature and like by the time I reached Year 10 I'd be fully mature and everything. And I'd lose my like funsense and stuff. My funsense, like, h-humour, humour! So I'd be like so serious and everyone else in the class would be so serious and we'd all have serious faces looking at the board working. But, I don't know if it's just my class in particular but we really haven't matured at all – I really don't wanna like grow up and then like become serious and everything it's like, you could be like 'hello Ierum' then be like (*Serious voice*.) 'hello'. And then they'd be like 'oh my god Ierum you're so serious'. I don't want to be like serious adult then have serious children and have serious future in a serious house and serious everything.

1.1.28. Moment of truth

LUAN*'s home. The table still has the tablecloth, this time with just a dish of salmon.*

AGRON. Yeah, happy new year! We had guests over and, um, they gone thank god. (*Chuckles.*) And Luan is on his toes today. We haven't opened his results so let's see. Can you bring the envelope, Drin? (*Beat.*) The moment of truth.

DRIN *gets the envelope and gives it to* LUAN. LUAN *opens it and peeps inside.*

LUAN. It's not the GCSEs.

LULJETA. Bear in mind this is not the final, it's the mocks.

LUAN *passes the envelope to* DRIN *who takes out the results. He looks at them and passes them to* LULJETA.

AGRON. What does it say, Drin? (*Pause.*) And?

LULJETA. Very, very, very bad.

AGRON. Is it?

LULJETA. Absolutely.

LULJETA *passes the results to* AGRON.

AGRON. Oh look you've got all red dots, man.

LUAN. It's cos my targets are high.

AGRON. What does a red dot mean?

LUAN. It means that I'm below my target, that's it.

LULJETA. It's the behavor.

AGRON. This is rubbish. Absolutely rubbish, look. It says here, end of tar– end-of-year target is six what you need to be and you / got three.

LUAN. For what? For English?

AGRON. Yeah. Yeah look, in everything of them. You don't have a B there you have all Cs and Ds man.

LUAN *takes the results.*

LUAN. I have a B, right here, I got a five.

AGRON. Where? Where do you / have five?

LUAN. Maths. Drin, is this a five?

DRIN. I'm not, I'm not gunna help you, / bruv.

LUAN. This is five for Maths. So Science I got a C overall, and you're telling me I can't bump it by one or two by the end of the year? / But I can. I know I can.

AGRON. Wha-wha-what makes you – what makes you think you will now?

LUAN (*emphatically*). Cos I can / I know!

AGRON. You let us down already once! You let down yourself!

Pause.

LULJETA (*to the audience*). Er, d'you-d'you like some salmon? Okay, wha' oo, my question is, what did you do the whole half-term?

LUAN. Nothing.

LULJETA. Why? Why? You know when you go straightaway you're gonna have the exams, why you never revised? Why? Why? You knew where you are!

AGRON. Pass me that paper again / pass me that pape–

AGRON *takes the results.*

LULJETA. Why am I gonna bother with you? You're not seven or eight-year-old, you are sixteen. Do whatever you wanna do.

AGRON. No it's not do / whatever you wanna do.

LULJETA. Oh yeah!

AGRON. No.

LULJETA. Oh yeah.

AGRON. It's my way or the highway / you understand.

LULJETA. Mmhmm.

AGRON. And he wants to go to a school in Rochester where they're all A, A, A-star students. How on earth you gonna get into with this result?

LULJETA. Obviously, we have to pay everything, for travelling, for food, for everything.

AGRON. / This is the result, if it was all A, / A, A, he would have got scholarship.

LULJETA. So, so.

AGRON. But because he hasn't got none of this 'good', so we'll have to pay for everything. He's not gonna get in. Not with this. Not with this, eh. (*Pause*.) It's not good Luan, it's not good.

LUAN. It's not that deep.

LULJETA *scoffs*.

AGRON. Is very deep, man.

Beat.

ACT TWO

1.2.1. Boys' Brigade service

A church, outskirts of Belfast. The BOYS *in the brigade huddle at the back of the church upstage, around the* BOYS' BRIGADE CAPTAIN.

The 'Colonel Bogey March' plays.

MARGARET. I think one of the boys, er, hasn't been able to make it tonight so they're having to rejig a few things and he's been asked to stand in for something he hasn't really hasn't really practised – so he's a bit uhhuhuh!

    CALLUM *and* JAKE *break away to talk to* MARGARET.

    You all ready?

CALLUM. Yeah, there's a, there's a big change cos one of our boys didn't show up, so yeah, I'll be in with the anchor boys, the two –

JAKE. We lost / Jesus.

MARGARET. Alright?

JAKE. Yep, Jes– Jesus ran away.

MARGARET. Oh dear. / (*Laughs.*)

CALLUM. In, in our performance. O' right, we better get back in.

    CALLUM *and* JAKE *join the rest of the boys in the brigade.*

BB CAPTAIN. Er, good evening everybody.

AUDIENCE. Good evening.

BB CAPTAIN. Good evening. You're very welcome to er – City Church, here to the er annual display of the eighty-first Belfast BB company. Erm, as you'll know this is the fiftieth, er, display – fiftieth anniversary – erm, a very special year for our, our Boys' Brigade company erm to have completed fifty years and it's wonderful that you're here this evening to be part of that and to share together in this, this celebration. Folks and boys keep that number going. Keep the light shining here. There's a family here and that family includes all of you and all the boys on the floor. And that's what church is all about. Church is about family. It's about fun, it's about family, and the third point we'll say is, it's about fellowship; our community, our city, our country needs Christian manliness displayed on a regular basis. This is where is starts.

'God Save the Queen' plays on the piano.

ALL (*sing*). God save our gracious Queen!
    Long live our noble Queen!
    God save the Queen!

1.2.2. Hug

School entrance hall.

IERUM *looks around, confused, trying to make sense of the map she holds.*

IERUM. So we've moved into a new building and it's really big, it's really pretty, I love it so much. Um, I don't know where to go, I really don't, like!

FRIEND 1. Ierum!

IERUM. I'm fine. Hello, hello, hello!

    Yeah, so –

FRIEND 1, 2 *and* 3. Ahhh hello.

IERUM. Hello! Yeah so I haven't seen my friends in, like, weeks so that's why they're all cuddly and hello-y to me, yeah. Sienna came and gave me a hug, she was like 'oh Ierum!' and I was like 'oh my god'. And I gave her a hug and I was really, really happy to see her.

    Yeah, so at the moment I'm just like trying to find my permanent spot. Like cos I can't just be jumping around like a rabbit, like a lost rabbit.

1.2.3. School council

Classroom.

CALLUM. Erm, it's good to be back, cos I love the school, like, you know, it's, it's like a second home to me, I just love it so, I was excited about coming back. For a couple of years, I used to think, well, wrestler, wrestler, wrestler. But now I'm actually coming to reality a bit for thinking yes, that would be good as a sideline but I'm not a fighter, I don't take pain very well. I think that this is a more career path for me. School council. I guess it's just wanting to make a change, you know, it's, may be, it's good to have that, kinda, power. I just get nervous about the whole thinking about it getting up in front of them.

The school council session begins.

MISS BRADLEY. Okay everybody, let's make a start.

CALLUM. Oh, here we go.

MISS BRADLEY. Okay everyone, so the first thing is, erm, the anti-bullying action plan. So, Callum, did you ever finish that?

CALLUM. I did indeed, yes, erm, so erm, I've got it with me, just in case you wanna look at it, but, erm –

MISS BRADLEY. If you just give everybody just a / brief overview that would be super.

CALLUM. Yeah, no problem. Erm so.

1.2.4. No Search

Classroom.

MIA. S'this is my third school now, if I get kicked out of here I can't go to another school. (*Beat.*) Casey, do you reckon they'll search you again today now no?

MIA *takes a tobacco pouch out of her pocket and hides it in her bra.*

CASEY. Probably after break.

Park.

MIA (*shouting*). KENDAL! (*Beat.*) Kendal!

KENDAL. We're not getting fucking / searched alright.

IESTYN. We're getting no fucking search.

KENDAL. They can't / search us.

IESTYN. Tell 'em to fuck off!

KENDAL. NO SEARCH!

MIA. No searches!

KENDAL. They need to ask our mum and dad because we're under the age of sixteen / so we're classed as a minor.

IESTYN. Yeah.

    KENDAL *and* IESTYN *start making a spliff.*

MIA. Wait no I'll put my jo– my song about Bethan Brice on:

She scrolls through her playlist on her phone looking for a song as she sings 'Shut Up' by Stormzy.

(*Referring to boys.*) Making a joint.

KENDAL. No we're not.

MIA. This won't get replayed to any of the teachers, you pricks.

KENDAL. Oh sound, yeah we're making a spliff.

MIA (*laughs*). Can I have a couple of drags of it please?

KENDAL. No.

MIA. Fuck yourself.

IESTYN. Blowback, blowback anyone / blowback blowback blowback?

KENDAL. I will

IESTYN. Do ya wanna see blowback? Iestyn blowback.

KENDAL. / Iestyn blowback.

IESTYN. It's called a Iestyn blowback. It's where you put a fucking fire / bit in your mouth.

KENDAL. Look.

IESTYN *gives* KENDAL *a 'Ieystyn blowback'.*

MIA. They're rare boys them.

KENDAL. Lovely. Lovely. Calmed my nerves completely.

IESTYN. Give it here.

MIA. I'm just checking my Snapchat so my Snapchat's not
   dead any more. (*Sings briefly. Spying a boy on her
   Snapchat.*) He is fucking bangable. (*Beat.*) Some lad on a
   picture, he is gorgeous. / He's tanned and he's got curly hair
   and I would / any day. Oh my god. (*Sings.*) – *holding the
   club an' the taste be like – damn.* I'd well cheat on Gavin
   with him.

IESTYN. I've got an old one so it's sound yeah.

KENDAL. Ah you bastard!

1.2.5. Wasn't feeling it

LUCAS*'s common room.*

LUCAS. So, I had grand plans. / (*Laughs.*)

BEN. Looking for a girlfriend. / (*Laughs.*)

LUCAS. Looking for a girlfriend um / and that did come –

BEN. Which succeeded, it did / come off.

LUCAS. Came round. Erm / and then, that was really good. /
   Um went really well. Today / I ended it.

   BEN *laughs.*

   BEN *laughs again.*

BEN. Today, it ended.

LUCAS. I finished it today.

BEN. Well.

LUCAS. Wasn't feeling it. (*Laughs.*) And, I'm – and it was sad.
   (*Laughs.*)

BEN. It's sad.

LUCAS. It was – it's very difficult. I've never, I've never properly broken up with someone and bloomin' hell. / (*Laughs.*) When you're face to face and you're – (*Exhales.*) But anyway, I enjoyed it while it last. It helped me through, you know, it was / um –

BEN. Hssss –

Good times.

LUCAS. Good times. But, you know, everything must come to an end.

BEN. Yeah, yeah.

LUCAS. And I wanted to do it sooner rather than later cos she's year above, so she's got her GCSEs.

BEN. Yeah, exact– so you don't want her to be / distracted / by you.

LUCAS. Yeah.

Distracted if I – yeah, I'm –

BEN. But it's her birthday / next weekend.

LUCAS. It's her birthday on the weekend. (*Laughs.*)

BEN. / So –

LUCAS. Oh god. (*Laughs.*) And I've bought her a present as well and I don't know what to do with it, it's sitting on my desk. I haven't told Teddy, my brother, because they're really good friends. They've known each / other since they were four. Ahhhhhhuhah.

BEN. Tuh.

1.2.6. Pepper plant

ROBYN*'s home*.

MIG. Jus' footed all / the debts.

ROBYN. Oh yeah, cleared, cleared the debts, had a lot of debt to pay Bridget as well that's all cleared I feel like a new woman. / (*Laughs*.)

MIG. She's cleansed! (*Laughs*)

ROBYN. Yeah, I've cleansed. I'd like to think I'm as good with money as Mum but I'm not… ss… but I do / have like her conscious around it, but I am quite bad with money, ss–, like Dad – (*Laughs*.)

MIG. I've had years of practice.

He's lovely, he's a lovely man your dad. He's just not good with money it just burns a hole in his pocket so I, I take charge. I always worry but we manage. And we manage because I'm… canny I suppose.

JAY *enters with a shopping bag and a pepper plant*.

JAY. Hi, how're you? I'm fine. / Sun's coming out.

MIG. / We send Dad to do the shopping.

ROBYN (*sniggers. Laughs*). Finally.

JAY. I'm just down to the shops, just to get it all out the way. As you do. Kind of got a pepper plant.

ROBYN. What?

MIG. Right, okay darling.

ROBYN. Ye– impulsive / buying.

JAY. I know it wasn't on the list.

MIG. Oh that's lovely, though, / peppers go'an – it's lovely.

ROBYN. Let me see.

MIG. It might not be an outdoor one. It might be indoors. It might be like the tomatoes. Check the wee –

JAY. Oh I wasn't thinking.

ROBYN. You do that a lot.

MIG. It's Daddy's impulse buying.

JAY. I have a bit of a weakness for bargains to be honest. And because I work in the city centre I've got lunch! Which lasts an hour. So I spend a lot of time popping into shops – just a wee look, as you do – um / but then you pop into TK Maxx and you see something that looks really good and you realise you're saving a hundred pounds! Even though you didn't want it, need it, or – but you end up walking out with it. So yeah I do that sometimes.

ROBYN *sighs affectionately.*

1.2.7. Who needs a father?

MIA. Gavin, he's officially moved into mine. In the trailer. Fuckin' – I don't even know what was going through my head. (*Beat.*) I've had like a month off because I couldn't be arsed coming in, my mum let me have like a month off. I think it's all the shit that's going on with my fucking prick of a father. I can't stand him any more. Got – he's – but he, he went to jail again, got released, again, and made a mug out of me again. Fuck – I'm done with him now, I've told him. (*Beat.*) Oh well. (*Beat.*) Who needs a father?

1.2.8. I'm shit-hot

Sports hall.

PATRICIA. Your situation now is the best Wales you've / ever done since being on board.

GEORGE. He said yeah hopefully in five years you might not even do it, ten years yeah, like you might actually realise how good you are and he wants you to say to Stu, yeah, 'Stu do you know what I'm actually not bad I'm shit-hot' yeah, and he said he hopes you do it but he knows you're so humble with yourself that you won't do it.

TAYLOR. No I just had an off game then. / No I genuinely did have an off / game.

PATRICIA. Y–

Did yeh? So you have one more game now, and you're coming home with a medal.

GEORGE. It's what I say boyo: 'let's fucking have it!'

1.2.9. New Year's revolations

Selfridges, Birmingham.

ALI. Oh, happy new year! I writ my, I writ down my er N-New Year's resolutions. Let me see, okay.

AYESHA. I haven't writ it, I'm not bothered. It's gonna be exactly the same as / 2017.

ALI. Okay, half of these haven't happened, okay. Pray five times a day.

AYESHA *chuckles.*

Revise for my ex– for my exams.

COUSIN 1. How's it going, Ali?

ALI. Be more organised. Stop eating junk food / (*Laughs.*)

COUSIN 1. Oh, oh that's not / happening.

AYESHA. Ohh.

ALI. Errrmm, look after my skin cos I have such bad acne. / And –

COUSIN 1. That's only because you eat junk food.

ALI. Stop talking to me to like half of the people I know. And focus on myself a bit more.

AYESHA. My New Year's revolation, whatever it's called, probably to, erm, make my mum proud.

ALI. Yeah. (*Gasps and claps.*) Pass my GCSEs that was one, another one.

AYESHA. After this shall we go Primark cos I'm feeling a Primark vibe, / and Boots…

ALI. I like Primark.

AYESHA. And Selfridges.

ALI. This is what Kim Kardashian wears all the time! This is their brand! Oh my god! (*Beat*.) So basically I'm Snapchatting the Yeezy collection that's in Selfridges.

ALI *and* AYESHA *take photos of the display*.

AYESHA. I just wanna Snapchat it so it looks like I got something on my Snapchat you get me, like?

1.2.10. Social media ensemble

Music plays. The youngsters move rhythmically around the stage, transfixed by their phones.

LUAN. Every day when I wake up the first thing I do is pick up my phone. See what's going on.

MIA. S'like I used to be able to wake up to like a hundred and twenty messages. Now I only wake up to like fifty.

ANNABELLA. I love my phone. So much.

AYESHA. It's my life. I'm not even / lying. It's got my whole life in it.

ALI. Exactly, yeah.

Oh my god / I wouldn't be able to live without my phone.

AYESHA. I'd probably die.

IERUM. A– if they'll, if phones weren't invented, it'd be more eashier for me.

MIA. I got nine'een likes on that.

ANNABELLA. If I didn't have a phone now then I'd feel really, like, like I didn't fit in.

MIA. Eighty-two on that.

ZAC. My Snapchat name, er, countzacula, I made it when I was a – twelve? Eleven.

MIA. Hundred and twenty on that.

ANNABELLA. It's a bit weird if you don't keep – if you don't have streaks, like I mean, just, like, everyone has them.

LUCAS. I used to do that loads, I had fifty streaks, an', that's ridiculous.

MIA. A hundred and three on that.

EMILY. Just like Snapchat, Facebook, Instagram. Just like, the classics.

IERUM. I don't really have Instagram and all them apps uhm because my phone isn't, like, an Apple phone.

ALI. I got my first phone when I was in Year 7. I got it as a reward for finishing the Qur'an.

MIA. Hundred and twenty-two on that.

CALLUM. Am I the only one that doesn't like that? You see if you think about things like that too much it can make really get to your head.

AYESHA. Sometimes at night, just to take pic-pictures I do my make-up. Just for a picture! (*Laughs.*)

LUAN. I think girls take it a bit more deeper than boys.

ROBYN. I have the most followers out of my friends. Apart from Lola, but Lola looks like a (*Laughing.*) model.

ANNABELLA. It's like this pressure to look like Gigi Hadid, 'ut's hard because, like, I don't. And, like, no one does.

TAYLOR. Twitter, I post everything on that, yeah.

LUAN. Your phone is like heroin right now, the fix! The fix!

MIA. I got nine'een likes on that.

LUCAS. Facebook. I sometimes stroll th-through the feed, when you're on the loo.

MIA. Eighty-two on that.

LUAN. Oh, I get depressed, like, I'm t-touching my pockets thinking where my phone is.

EMILY. In the day we're supposed to hand in our phones and then collect them at home time again. Like obviously, like, no one does it.

MIA. A hundred and twenty on that.

ROBYN. I'm not tethered.

IERUM. Who would have thought that a phone can be so important in my generation?

ROBYN. I feel like we're all batshit. Or maybe it's FOMO culture; we're constantly seeing what everyone else is doing so we wanna be involved, so we never get a break.

1.2.11. Culture and belief

IERUM. Like, everybody else is doing something that I can't do. All because of culture and belief. And my mum thinks that y– in her eyes I'm still a child and, like – so like, if I suddenly get the phone she'll just think that I'll be addicted to it but really I don't think I will cos I've witnessed a lot of children that are addicted to their phones. And I, I see, like, the impact and stuff. I can, I definitely know that's not really a good impact. And, I'm definitely not gonna be on a lot, I'm gonna move out and, like, live with myself and then save up money to buy my own phone.

1.2.12. The chickens have gone

EMILY*'s home.*

JEN *enters with a box of files that she sorts through.*

JEN. I don't know if Emily's told you, we're coming out of the boarding house. Yeah we've decided to come out early. So we'll go back to one of the villages. Yes, I think it will hi'er, hit her hardest because her social life's all here.

EMILY. I'm gonna be sad to leave. Um, yeah it's going to be like a lot harder socially. Cos obviously I won't be in Elland. (*Beat.*) Ah the chickens have gone, it's amazing. I'm so happy. I actually hated them.

JEN. Oh no chickens any more to eat all the leftovers!

EMILY. She used to cook extra for them.

JEN. No I didn't!

EMILY. Yes she did. (*Laughs.*)

JEN. As soon as she gets back from America she's, um...

EMILY. Someone's having / a party.

JEN. It's somebody's party.

EMILY. Thing is I missed Edith's party / because we were in Yorkshire and that was really unfair.

JEN. I know, the trouble is it's at Newmarket.

EMILY. Why is there no Wi– see there's no WiFi in this kitchen. It – Ah. I have a really itchy roof of my mouth I think I have hay fever. (*Pause.*) She doesn't care.

JEN. Oh dear, there's plenty of antihistamines upstairs.

EMILY. I've gotta be at a hundred per cent health so I can watch *Love Island*. / We all discuss who we like and who we think should be together.

JEN (*whispers*). Oh god. (*To* EMILY.) If only, if... only she knew her schoolwork as well as / she knew her – as my mother used to say 'Maa – if only you knew your schoolwork as well as everything else.'

EMILY. What are you talking about? I got five A-stars, five As and a B. No I got four A-stars five As and a B, / what you on about?

JEN. Alright. / I don't know.

EMILY. Yeah exactly. Which means all my predictions will be As and A-stars.

JEN. Ah, that's the one I'm / looking for, building; signed, sealed and delivered.

EMILY. She doesn't care.

She does not care.

1.2.13. Parents' evening

School hall. TEACHERS *are sat at individual desks which the* PARENTS *and* PUPILS *visit in turn.*

MR DAWSON. There may be some difficult conversations this evening because there are some concerns and in particular English, Maths and Science. And that is a concern. Cos I've experienced – as the director of learning for Year 11 – I've experienced defiance from your son, Luan. And, and I'm not appreciating that as the head of year. At / the moment, at the moment – sorry – at the moment your son is pushing boundaries. Just listen to the teachers, take on board what is happening because / all the teachers of Luan – no I know, no no, I know you are.

LULJETA. Yeah this, this was –

I do listen to the teachers and I do take on board!

That's fine.

MR DAWSON. Have a lovely evening, okay?

CALLUM'S ENGLISH TEACHER. Callum's excellent. He's great.

MARGARET. He, he loves English.

CALLUM'S ENGLISH TEACHER. Yes / I can tell.

MARGARET. He really really loves it.

CALLUM'S ENGLISH TEACHER. No, definitely. And it's reflected in your marks as well, so you target yourself an A, and in tracking one it got ninety-nine per cent and no one else got anywhere near that.

You're a delight to have in class.

MARGARET. Oh thank you very / much. (*Laughs.*)

CALLUM. Good, thank you miss.

ANNABELLA'S MATHS TEACHER. So… You look exhausted.

Pause. ALBERTA *wells up.*

Right, okay.

ALBERTA. I just pranged Mrs Teahan's car there, in the car park by accident when it was r– (*Chokes up.*)

ANNABELLA'S MATHS TEACHER. Oh no. You alright, do you want me to go and / get you a gl–

ALBERTA. Sorry for being / emotional.

ANNABELLA'S MATHS TEACHER. Nooo, no you're fine. Do you want me to go and / get you some water or something?

ALBERTA. I thought it would be okay. (*Sniffs.*) It's just come to me a bit of a shock. And she's like, don't worry it's just a scrape, it's fine. At least you told me, most people wouldn'ta told me and it's like, I couldn't live with that I have to tell, no way. I wouldn't like somebody to do it to me anyway sorry / irrelevant. Let's get back onto the subject.

ANNABELLA'S MATHS TEACHER. No.

Now Annabella. What's Annabella interested in doing next year?

ALI'S FORM TEACHER. So with regard to Ali, just sort of askin' him about how long he spends online on his phone. Social media's got a lot to answer for.

ALI (*sighs*). I hate school, hate it.

LUAN'S HISTORY TEACHER. All I see Luan doing is running round corridors, starting rows with Year 9 students.

LUAN'S ENGLISH TEACHER. I still feel like he's having too much fun and not taking the course seriously. Try not to smile too much when you're talking to me. / Driving me nuts.

LUAN. Alright.

LUAN'S SCIENCE TEACHER. He just don't do enough revision.

Beat.

LULJETA. I know that.

LUAN'S SCIENCE TEACHER. Um, in class he's very chatty. Luan has got exams in two weeks' time.

LUAN. Mm.

LUAN'S SCIENCE TEACHER. Let's see what Luan can do.

LULJETA. Every day we're gonna drop you at school and pick you up as a primary school.

ASIF. That doesn't sound very impressive.

LULJETA. / Exactly, thank you.

ASIF. You need to fix up, man.

LULJETA. You see? Asif is very good student. Did you do PE GCSE? / Yeah?

ASIF. Yeah.

LULJETA. And what did you get?

ASIF. I got a C.

LULJETA. C? / And do you know what Luan got?

ASIF. Yeah.

He got a C as well.

LUAN. Nah, I didn't get, I didn't get, I didn't get it.

ASIF. You didn't / get a C?

LUAN. That wasn't me, that was someone else.

ASIF. Oh.

ANNABELLA'S MATHS TEACHER. She has been forgetting books quite a bit recently. Er… she / h–

ALBERTA. I am tired of telling her to organise her books in the evening.

ANNABELLA'S MATHS TEACHER. Yeah, yeah.

ALBERTA. She is now fourteen. / She needs to just wise up.

ANNABELLA'S MATHS TEACHER. Yeah.

Yeah.

ALBERTA. And prove it herself.

ANNABELLA'S MATHS TEACHER. Yeah, yeah.

ALBERTA. It's just sloppy.

ANNABELLA'S MATHS TEACHER. Yeah, yeah.

ALBERTA. Sloppy? / Lazy? Sloppy?

ANNABELLA'S MATHS TEACHER. Yeah, yeah.

ALBERTA. Her head's gonna roll tonight. / (*Laughs.*)

ANNABELLA'S MATHS TEACHER. Yeah. (*Beat.*) Yeah.

So yeah.

ALBERTA. So don't – I'd, I'd never lift my hand to her just for the record but / but I'm just saying I am gonna give her such an ear-bashing.

ANNABELLA'S MATHS TEACHER. No that's –

LULJETA. Did you tell student what did they get?

LUAN'S PE TEACHER. Yes.

LULJETA. They did. So they know already?

LUAN'S PE TEACHER. Yep. (*Pause.*) Luan got a C… um and across the board – with the exception of one or two students – there was a bit of an underperformance.

LULJETA. I don't know what to say. You should have A-star.

LUAN. I passed it.

ALBERTA. Do you want to end up in a dead-end job, like soulless, serving people?

ANNABELLA. No / I wanna be a soldier, I'm not gonna / end up like that.

ALBERTA. Cos that's where you –

Right, well that's where you're going to go if you don't apply yourself.

ANNABELLA. No it's not.

ALBERTA. You have to apply yourself. When you're training you'll be learning how to use a gun.

ANNABELLA. Okay.

ALBERTA. You can't just decide 'oh I'll, I'll just put the magazine / I'll just put the magazine'–

ANNABELLA. That was Mrs Perkins over there, that was Mrs Perkins over / there for ya.

ALBERTA. Just put the magazine in later / when it suits Annabella, not when I have to / do it!

ANNABELLA. Yeah, okay.

Right, okay.

TASMIN. You know what? You need to sort your attitude out I'm gonna make him make you stay for an hour. Yeah. And I'm gonna say / sit her in the front – no –

AYESHA. No but check.

TASMIN. – No. There's nothing I can say good about you at the moment.

AYESHA. I am good but it's just teachers –

TASMIN. She's becoming – I can see her Jeremy Kyle in about ten years' time. / Innit probably having a few DNAs on her. /

ALI *laughs*.

ALI *laughs again*.

ALBERTA. Annabella, you're walking over me / I'm gonna go – ?

ANNABELLA. I'm sorry, Mummy, I didn't mean to be so / I –

ALBERTA. Cos you're on the phone.

Get off the / phone.

ANNABELLA. I'm getting off the phone.

ALBERTA. Give me the phone, I'm sick of your cheek. One week.

ANNABELLA. But I need to reply / to Lara.

ALBERTA. Tough. One week. Tough. I'm sick of your cheek.

ANNABELLA. Okay.

ALBERTA. Stop answering me back.

ANNABELLA. Okay.

ALBERTA. Stop it. That's her wee attitude, thinks she's clever. She starts on me when I'm not well, / I'm really not well.

ANNABELLA. I didn't mean to start on you.

ALBERTA. See what I mean? Stop it.

ANNABELLA. Okay, okay, okay I'm just –

ALBERTA. Answering back! Shush. Behave yourself. If you laugh at us I swear to god, I'll hammer you in front of everybody. See how smart y'are then.

1.2.14. Mum don't be angry

LUCAS. My main fear is just the, the day you get your results cos of – I've had it from both my brothers and it's all been happy, champagne for breakfast an', it's been lovely and I'm just scared that for me it's just gonna, people are gonna be like, 'Ah, don't worry Lucas'. I've – I've never worked before for anything and I have properly done stuff. I'm known in my fourth set as the, as the clever one; wahoo! Although, um, have got a girlfriend but she's o– she's great, I really like her. And, like, I haven't told my parents yet – (*Clears throat.*) cos (*Laughs.*) I don't know what they'll think. It – it's perfect, okay, tru– it is perfect, cos I work every single day I don't see her. Okay? And then in that afternoon that I see her that is my break for the week, okay? And you've gotta have breaks. Mum, when you're watching this (*Laughs.*) I – I did have a girlfriend during exams, don't be angry, okay? It was really good for me r-really helpful. (*Laughs nervously.*)

1.2.15. Happy Mother's Day

EMILY*'s home*.

JEN (*sings as she cooks*). Eurgh.

EMILY. Tired. Been working. Yeah just been doing some History.

JEN. Yes, still got a bit of French horn to do? / Um oh right okay.

EMILY. Yeah, I know I said I'm gonna do it this afternoon go away.

JEN. Oooo.

EMILY. Uh, just so – there's so much to learn.

JEN. Yeah I'm afraid it means sort of cutting back on all the enjoyable things for the moment, like all the young people do. Computing and TV / and what-have-you.

EMILY. Well I don't do that cos we don't have any WiFi so.

JEN. Right, did you want some of that bread? As well as the rolls.

EMILY. Just have a sandwich and some cake and some crisps literally like every other lunch.

JEN. Oh okay, well don't be grumpy, madam. Oh Emily I was going to put that nicely on a, on a m– thing, board.

EMILY. What?

JEN. The cheese and the ham / and stuff.

EMILY. Ohh we're not that posh. (*Beat.*) Can you pass me a piece of salami please?

JEN. 'Scuse / fingers. Um.

EMILY. Thanks. Er I had a Latin Literature and er I've got Maths next week, Geography next week, English Lang, Literature next week. Can I go work in my / room please?

JEN. You can go and work, I think we'll have a little amble while the sun's shining. Oh a bit of fresh air?

EMILY. No, no I need nooo, it's not funny I have exams. And I don't like allotments. (*Sighs*.)

JEN. Oh you can make us a nice cup of tea when we come back. / And some more cake. (*Laughs*.)

EMILY. No make your own tea.

JEN (*laughs*). It's Mother's Day! (*Hits the table four times*.)

EMILY. I don't care.

> JEN *laughs*.

Make your own tea. / I'm busy.

JEN (*laughs*). Urghhh.

1.2.16. Anxiety

ROBYN*'s home*.

ROBYN (*sighs*). Stressed. I've stopped job-hunting for the now cos of exa– everything's stopped because of exams, I'm just like in this horrible bubble but I'm – I decided that I'm gonna go out and find one as soon as they end.

MIG. Robyn's been quite anxious with / the exams.

ROBYN. Yeah. Not fun.

MIG. We've had some, mostly at night…

ROBYN. Yeah.

MIG. Wee panic attacks at bedtime and stuff like that, just kind of unhelpful thoughts crashing in.

ROBYN. Sometimes it just like it's just like a twinge in your stomach and you're like 'oh god I'm / gonna have one, soon.'

MIG. So it's just / anxiety and then it builds –

ROBYN. Yeah sometimes it's just anxiety and then sometimes like you know 'oh my god, I can't breathe, what the hell, I can't think any' oh my – it's like ho– it's like overwhelming, it is just overwhelming panic.

1.2.17. 32 GB

ALI *and* AYESHA*'s home.*

ALI. Today is my last, like, day in school, I just have to complete my cour-coursework for one subject next week. Do you know what I don't get? They make you remember so much things. And it's just like a waste of brain space. Yeah, like my brain's only thirty-two GB.

AYESHA (*laughs*). That's definitely me.

ALI. Shut your mouth. I can't wait to get my Eid clothes on.

AYESHA. Can't wait / until to get my ugly eyebrows done. So ugly (*Laughing.*) right now.

ALI. I got an exam in the morning though.

1.2.18. Line up

Outside the exam room. All the students are getting into line apart from LUAN *who sits on the ground.*

MR DAWSON (*blows whistle*). Can we please line up in our lines. Thank you.

LUAN (*to the audience*). My e– my exams so far have gone alright though, are you gonna be sitting with me in the hall, next to me?

MR DAWSON. Stand up. It's not appropriate, you've got an exam now, can you stand up. / You stand up. Stand up.

LUAN. My leg's hurting, sir.

  LUAN *eventually gets up and joins the line.*

  Music plays. 'Spring 1' recomposed by Max Richter –
  Vivaldi's The Four Seasons.

  Exam movement interlude. PUPILS *sat behind desks, sweating over their papers. The* TEACHERS *invigilate, walking up the aisles, checking up on them.*

1.2.19. Most valuable player of England

LUAN*'s home.*

The tablecloth is laid and there's a bowl of fruit.

LUAN. It went well, yeah. Yeah, it went well. (*Sniffs.*) Yeah.

AGRON. He studied hard. Yeah, no, he studied very hard and, er, and he put the work into it, he's been a good boy. Now we're just gonna wait for the results and if they're bad, dear oh me. Leg-breaker there. Leg-breaker. (*Laughing.*) Oh he won, look, look, look, (*Showing off* LUAN*'s trophy.*) 'English player' what they call, 'Under-Sixteen World Conference Dyman– Dynamic'–

LUAN. Most In– Most Valuable / Player.

AGRON. Most Valuable Player of England! Yes! Yeah! Luan! Yeah! / They didn't win the match though; runners-up.

LUAN. We didn't.

That / guy kills me.

AGRON. Runners-up. But he was the most valuable player because he scored fifty-three points, which is in basketball, amazing. But they're still losers. I mean they didn't win.

1.2.20. Happy with my nanny

On the way to a café.

ANNABELLA. I wa– I just wasn't happy at home. I wanna live with my nanny and, like, now I'm with her I'm really happy there and I just wish tha' like, my mum just, like, was happy with me staying there just being way, cos we argue too much. I just don't think my mum can, like, look after me that well, like, and I love being at my nanny's cos she irons my clothes and, like, um, she, you know, makes me breakfast and dinner and stuff, yeah and my mum, like, I re– I feel, like, really bad for her b'cos, like, now she's just really she's fallen out with me and she just doesn't want me back. She's taken me out of my will – er-her will. But I just want her to understand that I'm happy, you know, with my nanny and, like, I still wanna see her and all, but I don't think she wants to see me.

1.2.21. Darrell

Same set up as 1.2.19.

DRIN *enters*.

DRIN (*low-fives* LUAN). Did you win?

AGRON. Nah, man, they lost.

   DRIN *low-fives* AGRON.

DRIN. So you LOST?

LUAN. We lost.

AGRON. / It was close though.

LUAN. And then, they – they were giving the under-seventeen London regional letters. They gave one to Russell and Guy. Everyone was like, 'what? How come you didn't you get one?' Even the guy who got it said I should have got it, than him. Oh it was to play for the London team. And they just didn't give one to me. (*Pause*.) Bit / annoying.

LULJETA. What do you think about? Why didn't they give him one? I know why…

LUAN. Mum has / this, Mum has this, Mum has the worst – go on Mum tell your idea, she has the worst idea. Go on.

DRIN. I think he's just unlucky.

LULJETA. D'you want me?

LUAN. Yeah, 'oh his attitude's bad. He was being/ rude to te– the team'.

LULJETA. Yeah.

DRIN. Is that true?

LULJETA. No but I know Luan! He gets mad!

LUAN. That's not it, that's not / the reason!

DRIN. No it is true, it / is true.

LULJETA. He shouts / to the team. He gets mad, he – I know / him.

LUAN. Which –

DRIN. You seen the video? His highlights? Have you seen how every time he scores he walks off with a strut? He's like / (*Imitates strut.*) What is that man?

LULJETA (*laughing*). / Exactly.

DRIN. Just walk back to defence, man, there's no need to show off.

AGRON. No Luan / you're good man, don't worry. Study.

LUAN. Ah, move man.

DRIN. When's your next exam by the way?

LUAN. Um / (*Exhales.*) three weeks?

DRIN. You know Darrell, did you see Darrell before your exam?

LUAN. Yeah.

DRIN. So please explain to me why just before your exam as you're walking in you start shouting out towards Darrell, as if you're in like a pub or something, like 'Darrell, Darrell, ehh Darrell!' Why would you do that?

LUAN. Ah because we hadn't started the exam yet.

DRIN. But, was you walking inside the exam?

LUAN. No we / weren't.

DRIN. Yes, you was. You was in the line, / you at the back of the line…

LUAN. No we weren't cos I didn't see, I didn't see him when we were walking in.

DRIN. Why are you lying? / Do you want me to call him now?

LUAN. Were you there, were you there when we were walking in? Cos she were there with me.

DRIN (*to the audience*). Did you – did you see Darrell?

AGRON. So why you wi– er, you misbehave a lot, man?

LUAN (*grumbling*). / No.

DRIN. He does! Do you know what the teacher said to Darrell? He said, 'ah can you tell him' h'sai' – 'tell him, what, tell him to stop being annoying'. / What – why – why is he just telling Darrell?

LUAN. What? Where, where, where?

DRIN. Da', I'll call / him now, do you want me to call him now?

LUAN. Who? Wait, which / teacher?

AGRON. No, don't call him, man. Don't call him no.

LUAN. / Which teacher? Which teacher? Which teacher?

DRIN. I'll call him. No, I – I don't know what teacher.

LUAN. Was there any prob– did I get pulled out the line, Drin?

DRIN. What?

LUAN. Ah, did they / say 'go in office, you're not doing the exam'?

LULJETA. Was it any problem why he called his name?

DRIN. You don't / understand.

AGRON. What –

LULJETA. / What – what understand?

DRIN (*vehemently*). Why do you want your child before his exams to start shouting out someone's name like that?

LUAN. / Oh yeah.

LULJETA. / Alright.

DRIN. / Nah. / I don't care.

LUAN (*retaliating*). Cos you know what happens when you talk in the exam? Where you were? You don't understand what you're talking about / this.

DRIN. Oh my de– you're such an / idiot.

LUAN. No man, you don't know, you're an idiot, / move, you're telling me that I'm an idiot, / move, 'llow it.

DRIN. You're so stupid.

Do you know how many times I get people from the school /
telling me that you're always misbehaving?

LUAN. Yeahh. Yeah. Oh what did Mr Atkins say?

DRIN. Are you trying to tell me you don't get into trouble?
Don't sit here and tell me 'ah, I didn't get in trouble, I had
to – ' You know how you are in school, I know how you are
in school. / Don't try and act like you're not.

LUAN (*quietly*). Move, Drin.

AGRON. Even Darrell knows how you are in the school.

LUAN. Yeah.

1.2.22. Lighter with my name on it

A café. ALBERTA *and* ANNABELLA *sat at a distance from
each other.*

ALBERTA (*pause*). You'll need to come down next weekend to
look after the dogs, can I trust you to do that?

ANNABELLA. Yeah, of cou– yeah you can trust me to do that.
I swear cos I know you're not going to be there to look after
them. It's summer, so I have, I've got the time.

ALBERTA. No holidays for me, can't afford it.

ANNABELLA. I'm just back from my holiday to Salou.

ALBERTA. She better enjoy it cos that'll be the last one. So, I'd
spent six hundred pounds on new clothes for her and three
hundred euros so it was all in all about a thousand pounds,
give or take. Um, Annabella went to Spain, came back, and
bought me a lighter out of three hundred euros.

ANNABELLA. With, er, with your name on it.

ALBERTA. With my name on it. Out of three hundred euros.
Bought herself X amount of handbags, erm, and decided she
wasn't coming home so I went home to – I ended up trying
to get her home. Phoned social services. Social services said

to me, there's nothing they can do unless she's at risk. 'Is she at risk?' I says 'no, she's with her grandmother, she's fine, she's, she's fine, she's being looked after' so meanwhile, um, Annabella gets my mum to phone social services and tells social services my house is unfit to live in, it's filthy, it's stinkin', it's this and it's that. And she doesn't wanna live there any more. So I says 'right, I'll clean up me act, I'll sort me shit out', and, I says 'but she'll be coming home then?' So whether she wants to or not she'll be forced to come home. And if my mother dies in the meantime – which there's a high chance she will she's in her seventies – if my mother dies in the meantime, she'll be taken into care. You made your bed, you lie in it. (*Beat*.) So there you go, there's my news.

1.2.23. I won't help you any more

Same as 1.2.19 and 1.2.21.

LULJETA. I can't listen to this story, yeah, can you just stop?

LUAN. Thanks, Mum.

LULJETA. You trying to –

DRIN. You both know you / do it.

LULJETA. Trying to play an adult but you don't know, you shout at him.

DRIN. I can't – / I can't believe she just said that to me, you know? // How / is that right?

LUAN. Nah, Drin, you don't know, Drin.

LULJETA. I di– I didn't – I didn't.

LUAN. Why – why didn't you say that to me the other day? Why / didn't you just say that to me when you told me?

DRIN. Huh? Cos I forget, y– you're acting like – / Darrell told me and that was the number-one agenda for me here. Alright, cool, remember what I did for you, yeah? Remember what I did for you, then tell me if I don't care.

LUAN. Yeah cos you forget cos you don't care. You forget cos you don't care but if you did care to help me, if you cared to help me then you would have said something but you didn't. Clearly he snakes it, / but now that there's everyone here, now you don't wanna say it?

DRIN. Clearly I don't care, it's cool, it's cool.

I just want –

AGRON. Shu – shush.

DRIN. It's cool. Cool innit. I won't help you any more. / Fine.

LUAN. Okay. Thanks, Drin.

AGRON. That's what he wants.

LUAN. Yeah. Better.

AGRON. Really? (*Long pause.*) Was such a nice atmosphere, man. / Why did you come?

LULJETA. Exactly.

DRIN. Huh?

AGRON. Why did you come?

DRIN. I know, I'm leaving. I'm sorry I came.

AGRON. Just go man.

DRIN *exits.*

1.2.24. Half-tales

Same as 1.2.22.

ANNABELLA. I just don't wanna come home at the mo' when you're angry / and it's not gonna be pleasant.

ALBERTA. No it's good! No, it's fine, don't! She said something really sleaky to my sister and I didn't realise how, how I let it go unpunished. / She thinks she can get away with murder.

ANNABELLA. What? What? (*Pause.*) What did I say to your / sister?

ALBERTA. So there you go.

ANNABELLA. Mum?

Pause.

ALBERTA. About half a tale. Carrying half-tales.

ANNABELLA. Like what?

ALBERTA. I'm not getting into it with yeh.

ANNABELLA. I just wanna know / what I said.

ALBERTA. I already despise you enough.

ANNABELLA. I'm not coming home as long as you're being like that.

ALBERTA. You'll be made to.

ANNABELLA. Well, I won't.

ALBERTA. You will be.

ANNABELLA. I just wish you would / talk to me.

ALBERTA. Oh and it's all about your happiness, isn't it? It's all about you. (*Pause.*) So I'm about four weeks out of hospital. Two weeks out of hospital having to deal with this shit. (*She lights a cigarette.*) Excuse me for smoking, if you don't like it you can sit over there.

ANNABELLA. I just wish you would talk to me. (*Pause.*) So I do. Mum? Bu' she won't talk to me.

Pause.

ALBERTA. That's what happens when you report your mother to social services.

1.2.25. Ooh it's gonna be big

LUCAS. Er, summer holidays. Ooh it's gonna be big. Ooh. Erm, and I've got a party, I'm having a party. It's my birthday in three days! Oh, only like forty, which is lovely. Yeah, Mum doesn't want any more. Well she said thirty and I've invited forty s– and I haven't told her yet – so I'm – (*Laughs.*) It's gonna be fine, Mum, it's gonna be fine.

1.2.26. I'm so gassed

ALI *and* AYESHA*'s home.* AYESHA *admires her sparkling gold bracelet.*

AYESHA. Oh my god, I'm so gassed, I just finished my Qur'an, come home, and erm, it's crazy. Oh my god it's so nice!

UNCLE. Umbarakdisha, congratulations.

TASMIN. She's made more money that I make in a bloody year! Just on this one day what d'you get?

AYESHA (*laughs*). Loads.

TASMIN. That cost four hundred quid, just that bracelet. And / that's from me!

AYESHA. I – I – I'm I'm so (*Laughs.*) g-a-aassed! It's good, it's good I shave my (*Laughs.*) a-a-a-arms. / Yeah.

TASMIN. For finishing the Qu'ran.

AYESHA. For finishing the Qu'ran.

TASMIN. But I just need to take a picture, like, yeah? (*Laughs.*) That's my mentality, take a picture. Instagram's gotta have a picture. (*Laughs.*)

   TASMIN *gives her phone to* UNCLE, *who takes a photo.*

AYESHA. I'm so happy right now. It's like – it's like I've aplumplished something so long in my life. It's so nice.

ALI. Oh, I've started the gym, you know! Yeah! Pure Gym. Yeah, I love it. I wanna get such a nice body. So one day when I can go to the beach. (*Laughs.*) And just look so good.

1.2.27. Results

Projection on the back wall reads 'Results Day'.

TASMIN. Woooo! (*Laughs.*)

ZAC. It's (*Laughing.*) exam results today.

TASMIN. I'm more nervous that he is. (*Laughs.*)

TAYLOR. If I get a couple of Es and Fs I won't be too fussed about it.

TASMIN. I love you, liii.

ALI. Love you. Pray for me. Like what about if I fail?

TAYLOR. But then obviously I need to get into college to do sport.

ZAC. I – I'm feeling fine. Quite a lot of people don't have their results yet, like texts.

NAJMA. Literally it come – it could through at any time now.

LUCAS. I – oh god.

ALI. It's only a piece of paper.

LUCAS. You know, y– you – you just think the worst possible thoughts. That's just all you can think.

TAYLOR. It's like floating in warm water at the moment. Yeah, like, it could go west, yeah? So like a massive tsunami can just take me up and swallow me.

NAJMA. Why don't you have your phone, see cos I'm going to work in fifteen minutes.

ALI. I don't wanna go in.

TAYLOR. Scary shit, this.

ROBYN. I didn't get any sleep at all.

ZAC. I – I dreamt what I was gonna get.

ROBYN. An' then, I was like waiting for the postie. I was lying in bed, there / was chap on the door.

LUCAS. Derderderderderderderderder.

ROBYN. And I was like, 'Oh god.'

ZAC. Try and judge by my face if I have the results or not.

NAJMA. Oh come on!

   NAJMA *laughs*.

   No!

ROBYN. And I heard 'err SQA results?' And I was like, 'Eeeuuurghhhh.'

NAJMA. Right I'm gonna go off in a huff very soon.

ZAC. Yeah I actually, I actually have my phone on me. Messages...

ALI, ROBYN, TAYLOR, LUCAS *and* EMILY *open their results.*

ALI (*gasps*). Wait. Oh my god.

ROBYN. Ohhh my god!

TAYLOR. Look.

LUCAS. S-Spanish, Chemistry and Maths; three Bs. Sweet.

ALI. Oh my god, I got a one in Maths.

LUCAS. History A which is sweet.

TAYLOR. I got C in Gym so that's alright.

EMILY. I got ten A-stars and a B. Very, / very happy.

JEN *laughs.*

ALI. I've – uhm – passed English, I failed Maths.

JEN. And two were nines.

EMILY. That was in Maths and Latin.

LUCAS. Now then, starts getting decently nice now. Biology A, which is sweet.

ZAC. I did Biology and it was terrible.

LUCAS. Physics A.

ZAC. And I didn't – like I – cos I didn't really revise as much as I should have done.

LUCAS. Er Drama A.

ZAC. I was looking around everyone else and the teacher as like 'hrrrrhr' I was like 'okay'.

LUCAS. Art A.

ZAC. And I – what?

LUCAS. RS A-star and English Lit a nine.

ZAC. I'm just – I'm just saying this is (*Laughing*.) what happened.

LUCAS. Yes!

ALI. I feel like a twat.

LUCAS. And English Language a nine! Yes!

ZAC. And I was like 'yeah I failed that'.

ALI. I don't think I'm gonna get to do A levels.

ZAC. But I actually got a C in it. So – (*Laughing*) I didn't…

NAJMA. You didn't fail. Good.

ZAC. Whoop – then I got As in everything else.

NAMJA. Well done. Woo!

ZAC. Wow!

LUCAS. Oh, come on. So yes. Ah – yeah. Oh. Ooh.

NAJMA. Zac, that's brilliant! We know Biology wasn't your strongest subject.

ZAC. Why you focusing on the negatives?

1.2.28. What do I stand for?

LUCAS*'s part song rehearsal.* BEN *stands in front of the piano.*

BEN. Right, do we know our notes for the…?

A chorus of 'yes' and 'no.'

LUCAS. Erm, actually, can we just go over my um-bop before I –

BEN. Yeah, er, what are you? Are you? –

LUCAS (*sings*). Ummmm.

BEN. Okay you're at – (*Sings*.) U/mmm bop, doop bop bop, ummm –

LUCAS (*sings*). Ummmm bop, doop bop bop, ummmm.

Let's do it.

SEB. – Really loud, really energetic.

BEN (*hammers piano*). Lucas!

BEN *plays the opening notes and they hum to find their starting note.*

One, two, three, four.

They sing the first verse of 'Some Nights' by fun., a cappella, then gently hum under the dialogue.

ANNABELLA. When's Brexit day? Why are we leaving the EU anyway? It's going to be so hard to travel, ugh, ridiculous.

LUCAS. Yeah, well, I was remain. My whole family were remain. I'm worried for my later life. It's gonna be really hard.

EMILY. I just – I just think it's a really dumb idea to leave. It's like all the really old people who voted out and they're just all gonna be dead soon.

ZAC. Also see UKIP right, so their, their whole thing was like, 'we want independence for like "UK".' They've got it, why are they still here?

TAYLOR. Wait, Boris Johnson's Conservative, yeah? Oh, he's a knob'ead him, yeah. Aren't they supposed to sell the NHS and all that as well? To the US yeah? NHS goes, yeah, I'll have to, like, be in a wheelbarrow or summin.

CALLUM. Now I'm not a huge fan of Boris. I don't think many people are to be honest with you. Ultimately, I'd prefer a new leader, but, you know what it's the best we've got right now. And at least now we're kinda going for Brexit now.

AYESHA. I would so run the country better. Imagine I should run for presiden– president / or?

ALI. Prime Minister.

AYESHA. Prime Minister.

ANNABELLA. I think James Cordon should be Prime Minister. I just think he's such an amazing guy.

They sing another verse then return to humming under the dialogue.

ROBYN. And we watched the election all night. Oh (*Retches.*) I voted for SNP. Even as a political person I'm sick of it. Can we just burn parliament, already? I'm done w'it.

MIA. I don't understand it. I'm not into politics it's confuses me.

LUAN. I'm – I don't need to vote. It's not really my problem.

IERUM. When I'm older, if like, I didn't achieve all my dreams, then when I'm older I wanna like help other people see the world the same way that I do. And then maybe make the world a better place.

They sing again, finishing the song.

First interval.

PART TWO

ACT THREE

2.3.1. I've flopped

AGRON*'s car. He is driving,* LUAN *sits behind,* DRIN *is in the passenger seat.* LUAN *holds his GCSE results.*

LUAN. Yeah so um, I've, I've – I've got in to Leyton, the other one but I'm going to Rochester County High to see if they give me like be'er options then I might go County High. But I haven't decided yet. Leyton, Leyton's the one – basketball-wise – is better, but County High academic, academically it's better as a school, I reckon.

AGRON. No but the schools you gonna need to get into they're not offering what you want.

LUAN. Yeah-they did, Leyton's jus' offered what I wanted.

AGRON. Well, yeah exact – Philosophy, when did you want to study Philosophy?

LUAN. Ah, am I doing Philosophy?

AGRON. Yeah, that's what you said, / they offered you Philosophy.

LUAN. Ahhh. No, I'm not / doing Philosophy.

AGRON. You don't even know what Philosophy is.

LUAN. I'm not doing Philosophy, / Drin.

AGRON. What is Philosophy Luan-Din?

DRIN. He's not doing / Philosophy.

LUAN. I'm not doing / Philosophy.

AGRON. But that's what he said to me.

DRIN. Nah, he said Sociology.

AGRON. Sociology?

DRIN. Which is worse.

AGRON. Ah. Why don't you be a doctor / Drin-Luan?

LUAN. BTEC Sports. (*Smacks lips.*) Oh man, I flopped.
(*Laughs.*) I should have put better options, damn.

DRIN. If he goes here then he has a reason to actually do well.
Cos if you (*Smacks his leg.*) come here, and they're paying
(*Smacks his leg.*) accommodation for you to get (*Smacks his
leg.*) Cs; ssshh.

LUAN. Nah, the school's sick, Drin.

AGRON. Don't come back.

DRIN. Boy, ah (*Smacks his leg.*) stay there, / amazing.

AGRON. And you're lucky because basketball gets you up
here –

DRIN. / Yeah.

AGRON. Wherever you're aiming because the guy, the coach,
wants you / whatsoever.

DRIN. Yeah.

LUAN. I know, I'll just chat to the coach before we go in / an'
be like.

AGRON. No, you don't chat; / you talk.

LUAN. Talk.

AGRON. By the way this guy takes them November to USA.

DRIN. Really?

AGRON. An' that'll cost me three grand.

LUAN. See? Oh my god, no way. This is another reason why
I don't wanna come here. (*Beat.*) I've got, er, I got, I got, um
called, I got called up for the Kosovan national team. Like
yeah, so then –

DRIN. Do you have time?

AGRON. / Yeah.

LUAN. Yeah I wanna go play for Kosovo… and repres– and represent the country.

DRIN *taps his legs and claps his hands and* LUAN *laughs.*

AGRON. I'd, I'd like him to represent England.

LUAN. Nah / leave it, leave it, / wow!

DRIN. Wow!

AGRON. He grew up here man!

LUAN. Na – / (*Laughs.*)

DRIN (*taps his legs*). / Wow.

AGRON. What?

LUAN. I'd rather represent Kosovo, I'm not gonna lie.

AGRON. You serious?

DRIN. / Oh my days.

LUAN. Yeah, I don't know why I'd rather represent Kosovo.

DRIN. I am shocked. As someone who tries to, to make sure we are raised in a Kosovan / environment so we know our culture, you know, patriotic.

AGRON. Yeah but you're, you're done enough, you've done enough.

LUAN. Naah, I feel more proud playing for Kosovo.

DRIN. Definitely.

AGRON. Do you really?

LUAN. / Yeah, I actually want to, I don't know why.

DRIN. Yeah, of course, of –

AGRON. You but born here, man!

2.3.2. Bumped up

EMILY's home.

EMILY. I got my French bumped up to an A – (*Beat.*) So I got ten A-star and A not a B. I was one mark off and I got it bumped up which was quite good. I was looking on like York, Edinburgh and Newcastle. Cos I definitely want to, I don't want to go Oxbridge no way, I'm not clever enough to.

2.3.3. Ofsted distinction

Outside County High School.

LUAN. What d'you think, Drin?

DRIN. Mad.

AGRON. I've heard their, their, Ofsted is distinction. An' again it's very high.

DRIN. So are we allowed, are we allowed to go in?

AGRON. I, I dunno.

LUAN. Drin, come with me. I'm bringing you.

AGRON. Yeah. You go / with –

LUAN. Definitely, definitely come with me. Don't leave me alone / me and Drin'll go in.

DRIN. We'll see.

I can't help you.

AGRON. You need to improve your accent if you come / here.

LUAN. Who me?

LUAN *and* DRIN *exit tentatively.*

2.3.4. Driving lessons

Same as 2.3.2.

EMILY *opens an envelope.*

EMILY. What's this?

JEN. It might be your provisional driving licence.

EMILY. Yeah boys.

JEN. Hmmmm.

EMILY (*reads from the letter*). Learning the official DVSA. I'm getting driving lessons for my birthday. Erm – we swapped our seven-seater for a Ford Fiesta. So I want to pass as soon as possible cos if you don't do it in the lower sixth you literally don't do it until you're thirty. So, I want to get it done, as early as possible preferably before sixth-form exams.

Can I drive, ah can I drive to school on the first day?

JEN. No, you can't.

EMILY. Why not / I'll be seventeen? /

JEN. You have to have – yeah but you have to have some lessons first –

EMILY. Yeah sure –

JEN. Before you drive just out on the road like The Wild Thing.

EMILY. Not if you go in the automatic car I'll be fine. Can you feed me I'm hungry?

JEN. Can't cook a chicken nugget but she's gonna be allowed to drive is a rather / worrying scenario.

EMILY. I'm hungry.

2.3.5. Very proud of myself

ALI *reads from his acceptance letter.*

ALI. Dear Ali, congratulations we are delighted to be able to offer you a place at Thomawo–, Thomas Attwood Sixth Form College for September two thousand and eighteen. (*Pause.*) I'm very proud of myself and everyone's very proud of me.

AYESHA. I'm not.

2.3.6. A fresh of breath air

Same as 2.3.3.

AGRON. Did they offered you a place then?

DRIN. W-w-w-w it looks like it, yeah.

AGRON. Oh, what you mean it looks like it?

DRIN. Um he has to ask for Business but the – I think the chances are they'll let him do it.

AGRON. So what, what you doing then, Luan?

LUAN (*sighs*). Um.

DRIN. Business, Applied Science and, er, / Sports Science.

LUAN. Sports Science.

DRIN. Which is actually pretty good.

LUAN. Oi, you lot, I actually wanna come here but I don't.

AGRON. You don't wanna come? / You don't wanna come?

LUAN. Er, don't know.

DRIN. Th-they all think you're coming mate. / They're all waiting for you like!

LUAN. Yeah that's the bad thing. (*Beat.*) Ah, you lot I don't know what to do.

Drin, Drin.

DRIN. What?

LUAN. If you had the option right now, who would it be?

DRIN. Luan, if I was in your shoes right now / I'd be...

AGRON. Shall we get something to eat, is everyone hungry? Yeah we'll stop in Asda's and have a d– / a fresh pasta.

They get back in the car.

LUAN. Drin, help me would you?

DRIN. I'd get home and start packing my bags.

/ AGRON laughs.

LUAN. What, you fully go (*Claps.*) County?

DRIN. Yeah, man.

AGRON. / Drin, man, I love you.

LUAN. Ah, say no more, I've decided.

AGRON. So this is a fresh of breath air. This is a fresh of breath air.

2.3.7. New watch

CALLUM*'s home.* MARGARET *holds his blazer.*

GRANNY. Now don't be going down and getting girlfriends just because you're in fourth form – not happening.

CALLUM. I'm not, Granny.

GRANNY. Okay.

MARGARET *hands* GRANNY *her camera and helps* CALLUM *into his blazer.*

MARGARET. Gonna get a picture.

GRANNY. Get a picture.

CALLUM. I'm putting my blazer on.

GRANNY *takes a photo.*

GRANNY. You're right my camera is rubbish.

MARGARET *laughs*.

MARGARET. Are you wearing your watch today?

GRANNY. Ah. (*Clears her throat.*)

MARGARET. He got himself a watch over the summer now
coz he never wears a watch and – and then he's got it to wear
and now he's going ooooh / I don't like it on.

GRANNY. Get it on.

CALLUM. That's not true – I jus'-I think I might go the first
day without it – / (*Beat.*) So I can actually –

GRANNY. No, no put it on the first day you'll be, you're in the
fourth form put it on the first day. I insist, we had how many
minutes to stand for you choosing that watch?

GRANNY *puts* CALLUM's *new watch on him*.

MARGARET. He's very indecisive.

GRANNY. And hasn't he got tall I swear I'm either going down
or you're definitely going up and the feets getting bigger as
well.

MARGARET. I know.

CALLUM. I'm just excited to go to my classes, see my teachers
and get, you know, books and stuff. You know the new books
so.

2.3.8. Go America

AGRON's *car*.

AGRON. You going to school in High County, man! Tell 'em /
I'm posh now.

DRIN. County High!

AGRON. County High. Tell them I – you're, you're posh now.

DRIN. You're gonna meet, er, you're gonna meet different
types of people.

LUAN. Yeah, they're all gonna be dull and…

DRIN. / Nah.

AGRON. You're gonna meet progressive people.

DRIN. / Yeah.

LUAN. They'll all be smokin' weed.

DRIN. Nah, nah where you are now, that's, they don't smoke weed they sell it.

LUAN. Hey Dad's (*Claps*.) gass'd, Dad's gass'd! Dad's gas! You got me out the 'hood.

DRIN. Ha-ha-ha.

AGRON. Finally. (*Beat*.) An' listen, go America. Go / America. Man! America. About three grand. We'll raise it together won't we? We go in a, in a farmers' market and sell some honey an' stuff, don't worry. And I'll play Lottery every week.

2.3.9. Trustworthy guy

LUCUS's *bedroom suite at school*.

LUCAS (*animated*). So I'm in a two-bedroom suite with Kemi umm with our desks, desks in it. I have a bed looking out over, over the garden and the town which is lovely. I-uhm-I'm-I'm in a relationship – I know how fancy, yeah. But Georgie, Georgie's going strong, we like Georgie.

KEMI *enters*.

Ah hey Kem.

KEMI. Hello –

LUCAS. And I trust myself fully. I trust myself completely and I'm a very trustworthy guy –

KEMI *clears his throat*. LUCAS *gives him a sideways glance*.

– but if I, when I, I might not be seeing her for like two months and I have parties back-to-back. (*Sigh*.) I'm gonna be fine; I'm gonna be fine.

2.3.10. We're having photos

IERUM'*s school hall.*

Pupils mill around and line up for photos.

IERUM (*panicked*). Photos!

KIRSTY. Yeah I know / I didn't even do my hair.

IERUM. We're having photos! I did not know that! (*Beat.*) Oh my god I didn't know – ha! We're having photos apparently. Oooooh. I hope I look nice. Kirsty, Kirsty how do I look?

KIRSTY. Huh.

IERUM. How do I look? Like. Don't / lie.

KIRSTY. Y' look nice, you look really good, you look stunning woman, stunning.

IERUM. Ha ha. I didn't do my hair nice or anything.

KEISHA. It's the first day of school how did you not know something was gonna happen.

IERUM. I did not know nobody told me!

2.3.11. Rejected

ROBYN'*s home.*

ROBYN. We didn't go away this year. Ah – we just had to – we had to buy a boiler this year (*Laughing.*) so it was either a boiler or a holiday so (*Laughing.*) we got a boiler. (*Beat.*) I've literally I've been applying for jobs for four days now.

JAY. Good.

ROBYN. I've got two comebacks but like two jobs that are like interested in me. One is at the Forge Shopping Centre though.

JAY. Okay.

MIG. That is good.

ROBYN. Yeah that's fine and like.

JAY. It's the law of average though isn't it. I mean you just have to keep applying.

ROBYN. Yeah.

JAY. That way I can stop giving you pocket money.

Laughter.

ROBYN. Oh yeah no I've applied three times bu' it's really difficult it's really hard to work for McDonald's. They're really strict. You need Nat 5 Maths. Something which I do not have.

MIG. You need a Nat 5 Maths to work at McDonald's?

ROBYN. You need Nat 5 Maths to work at McDonald's. It was just a cashier but there was like forty-three pages I had to go through to even apply for it not even get it, to apply for it. I'm sorry but I do not need to speak Arabic to hand out Chicken Selects!

JAY laughing.

I got rejected from KFC and Pets at Home in like the same week. I'm a young youthful face in the business why won't you employ me?

2.3.12. Jeff Bezoz

Same as 2.3.9.

LUCAS. I'm doing some ww-ork experience with a friend er who's in the property business in London. Doing some more work experience in er John Lewis with a bit of retail. I know cos aaa – friend, he's big in that and then I might do some stuff with Dad but his company don't offer work experience so he'll only be able to get me in for like, a couple of days maybe. Just stop off at some of his meetings, he's, he's very busy at the moment got a, got a promotion so he's all. – Working with Jeff Bezos next week. Amazon, richest guy in the world. Apparently, he's a weirdo though Jeff Bezos, he's done some weird stuff.

KEMI. Like what?

LUCAS (*laughing*). Think if – if you search up Jeff Bezos some dodgy stuff comes up and I know he's been in the lews a lot.

KEMI. / Sexual?

LUCAS. But yeah I think so.

KEMI. Oh, fuck.

LUCAS. Yeah, he's like, I think he's got like ninety bill yeah, so he's doing quite well Jeff Bezos, ma man. Can we get Dad to ask for free Amazon Prime. (*Laughs*.)

2.3.13. Like Minecraft

Same as 2.3.10.

KIRSTY. Do you know like, ya know like Minecraft.

IERUM. Yeah.

KIRSTY. That's what it looks like. Your face looks all pixelated.

IERUM. Oh my god that's so bad! Oooooooh I don't want to do, I really don't wanna do thit. Ah. I'm not lookin' at the mirror, I really want to look at the mirror. Alright. (*Squeals*.) I don't wanna do it any more.

KIRSTY. Just do it.

KEISHA. Just do it!

BOY. It's a photo Ierum.

MRS JONES. Surname madam?

IERUM. Hakim.

MRS JONES. H A K I – It's a selfie so I'm going to let you take your own picture okay.

IERUM. Alright. Okay.

IERUM *takes the selfie*.

Oh my god my skin's really dark.

MRS JONES. No it's not, it's just the camera. Happy with that one?

IERUM. Umm (*Beat*.) no.

MRS JONES. RE-take then?

KIRSTY. Right. That was bad.

MRS JONES. Press the button. Lovely.

IERUM *takes another selfie*.

IERUM. Oh my god I look like, I was like sunburnt. Is my skin actually that dark?

2.3.14. Love my new school

ANNABELLA*'s home*.

ALBERTA. Much better with Annabella. Things have been much better. Less attitude, closer than what we have been. (*Referring to Peg, her dog*.) Don't worry if she cocks her leg on you, she won't pee it's a wee nerve thing. Well she moved schools, see since she moved school, different child.

ANNABELLA. Ah I actually love my new school so much.

Beat.

ALBERTA. What she's done?

ANNABELLA. Mmm?

ANNABELLA *sees that Peg has gone to the loo on the carpet*.

Argh, / Peg!

ALBERTA. Stinker. You're a dirty / dirty girl.

ANNABELLA. Jesus Mum.

ALBERTA. She's a cheeky dirty, isn't she, / disgusting.

ANNABELLA. Yeah. But um no I'm really really happy where I am. I'm doing Science. It's actually really good, and everyone there is so nice and I've made new friends and everything an' just / (*Pause*.) really good.

ALBERTA. / really good. I know, it's far better.

ANNABELLA. But everyone at my new school like they're just so nice. Everyone'll smile at me being like, 'oh you're so pretty' and 'oh I really like your eyebrows and 'oh my gosh' and 'blah blah blah' and 'where do you come from?' and it's like I just felt so welcome and I feel like I really fit in.

2.3.15. Shotput's taking over

Sports stadium.

TAYLOR. Yeah, so basketball's becoming more of a hobby of mine as shotput's taking over and my shotput coach said because if I want to go far with shotput I'm going to need focus on it a lot more. Hopefully go to the Olym– Paralympics in Tokyo.

PATRICIA. So yeah we're just here because it's, it's the pathway, an' you know what we're like as a family when somebody says, 'come an' ha' a go', we'll try it, we like it we don't yeah. To be fair this is the first time he's been up against men.

GEORGE. We were told Tay' if Taylor would have gone to the Europeans last week yeah he'd have come home with gold /

PATRICIA. / gold

GEORGE. Cos he beat the guy who won there by / twenty centimetres.

PATRICIA. Just in practice, I know.

GEORGE. Jus' practisin'. So he's / got the capability yeah.

LEENA *enters with refreshments.*

TAYLOR. It's Leena, my girlfriend.

PATRICIA. Too long, / yeah together? (*Laughs.*)

TAYLOR. Two, yeah, two / years an'…

LEENA. Yeah. Fed up now. Jokes. Not really. / (*Laughs.*)

PATRICIA *laughs.*

TAYLOR. Two years and something / months.

PATRICIA. Is it? Is it two years, yeah? (*Exhales.*)

TAYLOR. Quick, / yeah.

PATRICIA. No wonder I was panicking about babies here, Leena?

TAYLOR *laughs*.

PATRICIA *laughs*.

LEENA. No thanks.

2.3.16. Finished with Gavin

MIA. I finished with Gavin. I have a future. I had a hell of a good summer, just did what I wanted and that, yeah. And then this boy started messaging me and he was twenty-two and I was only sixteen so I used to ignore him, and then when I turned seventeen I was like 'oh it's not that bad it's only like five years' there's something like that between my mam and my d– er, between my auntie Amanda and my uncle JD yeah, so I was like yeah sound, sweet, whatever, yeah.

2.3.17. Hot Cory

ROBYN. Oh god, this one guy, this one guy did have like a thing for me and I was like 'dude' cos he was, his literal nickname was 'Hot Cory' and I was like 'man! Man! Good shit' and my mate Hamish was like 'yo, Cory Campbell' I was like 'yeah'. He was like, 'right well he has a thing for you' I was like 'ah man, that's pretty chill' when Hamish comes out with 'yeah but I told him you were a lesbian because I don't think he's your type'. I was like 'Hamish! You piece of shit'. It's turned out so badly. Devastated. I didn't even like him, I just was like well he's hot and he likes me this is great, this is the ego boost I've needed for (*Laughing.*) years!

2.3.18. Stress

ZAC*'s home*.

ZAC. I've got umm like red all round my, I get like rashes. No, I don't know it's from something, but I just get really bad. Sorry my eyeballs – (*Laughs*.)

NAJMA. We're gonna have to get him some cream. You know what my, my take on it is, as mother: he's very relaxed, very chilled boy / er but here's my take is your body, cos the body's gone / enough.

ZAC. Yess.

I think-it, I think it's stress.

NAJMA. Okay I didn't want to use that word but – (*Beat*.)

ZAC. My umm my hair, when I was in Germany actually the first few days I would like go like this and I would just have like / so much hair in my hands.

NAJMA. Oh no / oh no that's stress.

ZAC. Did I tell you that and I woke up, I wake up in the morning and my pillow was covered in hair.

NAJMA. That's disgusting.

ZAC. Yeah but I-I didn't feel stressed but it's where my body telling me – you're stressed.

2.3.19. Proper glowing on Eid

AYESHA *sits in the beauty parlour, the* BEAUTICIAN *readies his piercing gun*.

AYESHA. Me I like to look like proper glowing on Eid innit.

BEAUTICIAN. Right.

AYEHSA (*on phone*). I dunno.

BEAUTICIAN. Are we ready? Okay are we doing it there?

COUSIN 1. Get off the phone then.

AYESHA (*on phone*). She did my forehead, upper lip and eyebrows for five pounds. I gotta go they're gonna just pierce my nose right now, Khatimi.

BEAUTICIAN. Gonna serve some customers. No, no you need to get off the phone.

AYESHA (*on phone*). Rania I'm gonna get off the phone, bye.

BEAUTICIAN. Any time, errr – new kids. This new generation man, got stuck to their phone. (*Beat.*) Right I'm just gonna line it up. I'm just gonna check –

He pierces her nose.

Done. There we go.

AYESHA. Aahaaaa.

BEAUTICIAN. That's it, that's how we do 'em.

AYESHA checks herself in the mirror.

AYESHA. Oh my god I like it.

BEAUTICIAN. Yeah

AYESHA. I love it.

BEAUTICIAN. Thank goodness for that.

AYESHA. Thank you so much.

BEAUTICIAN. You're very welcome, sister.

AYESHA (*kisses her lips*). I look so good in Eid pictures.

Laughter.

2.3.20. I'm not pretty

IERUM (*tentatively*). So, mm, as I got older I started realising that, you know, um, I'm not really, like, I don't know I just feel like… I'm not pretty. Yeah. I, I, jus' – I don't know I just, just started thinking about how I looked. And looked at myself in the mirror. Um, I just then noticed that… I should lose weight… because… I jus' – I don't know, I just started thinking that suddenly after seeing – noticing – that all my friends are, like, really… n-nice, and they're, like, pretty.

And when we went into the sports hall, I – cos we have like really big mirrors – and then I just noticed a huge difference between me and them. I'm trying to, like, become someone who's pretty. I don't – I don't know, I started doubting myself. And that's when I started eating less in the holidays. And I started, like, starving myself.

2.3.21. Massive self-image issues

ROBYN. Like I had massive self-image issues for so long as a kid. I mean I was a fucking ugly child but that's not the point. I was like really insecure for so long and I hit puberty and I was like 'where is it'ss'nothing's happening?' And then my mate Bridget was like 'you're a fucking idiot you're really gorgeous' I was like 'ohhh!' Cos she's like super pretty so when she said – and she has also got massive self-image issues – me and Bridget are just hopelessly lonely. (*Laughs*.) We're just like I haven't, I haven't been in a relationship for so long! I would just like somebody – or a girlfriend I don't mind – I identify as (*Laughing*.) bisexual. I c– I – I've always had like an inkling but like there was like some slight confusion I was like 'oh wait, what is it? What am – I'm not, not sure' and then when I was thirteen I was like, 'oh wait that's what it is, okay, that makes a lot of sense'. My parents: 'yeah we fucking know' I was like 'oh great!' (*Laughs*.)

2.3.22. Self-image ensemble

Music plays. The youngsters vogue to the music as they scrutinise themselves in an imaginary mirror.

AYESHA. I hate stuff about my face. My eyebrows –

ANNABELLA. See sometimes I look really really young.

AYESHA. My forehead.

ANNABELLA. Like if I don't have my eyebrows on.

AYESHA. My nose.

ANNABELLA. Or I have like my hair in pigtails and stuff.

AYESHA. My lips.

ANNABELLA. I just look like a baby.

AYESHA. My teeth.

ALI. Your whole face basically.

AYESHA. My cheek. Yeah basically I hate my whole face.

MIA. My eyebrows are too big.

ALI. I want er – a better hairline I feel like it's going back.

MIA. My eyebrows are not on fleek.

ZAC. I don't know that's human nature really. You know you're not happy with what you've got.

AYESHA. I'm going to get fillers in my cheek.

IERUM. Oh my god, I look like I was like sunburnt.

AYESHA. My eyebrows microbladed.

ZAC. The grass is always greener and all those other quotes, what's the Joni Mitchell one?

ALI. And I kind of hate my nose but then I like it sometimes.

ZAC. You don't know what you've got till it's gone. Yeah, music degree!

AYESHA. An' then get a hairline reconstruction or whatever it's called because I need to look peng when I'm older.

CALLUM. But you shouldn't alter yourself just to, to appease others. You've just gotta be secure in who you are.

LUCAS. I really want an eyebrow piercing and I want a buzzcut.

ROBYN. I want people to look at me and be like ah that's cool but aside from that no I don't give a fuck.

LUAN. I'm feel like I'm very comfortable in what I wear. Just anything really I don't really think it's that deep.

IERUM. Well I wish I was like that but ah. I'm really picky.

ROBYN. You've got to like form a sense of self.

EMILY. Like we were going to like the winter ball last year and I was-I was with a bunch of people before and they're like are you wearing gold or silver jewellery and I didn't realise that people used to wear like all gold or all silver and I've started doing that since then cos I used to just wear mix and match and then I realise like people don't do that.

ROBYN. Like all those people who bullied me do not have what I have and what I have is a sense of character and a sense of self so who's, who's the real fool?

TAYLOR. I love myself yeah. I'm a decent-looking lad ya know, look at me instead of the chair first.

ROBYN. Stand there and be like listen all you bitches with the H&M skinny jeans and fake tans and you say the N-word despite being white yeah you ain't, you ain't gonna be shit.

2.3.23. Workout videos

IERUM. My mum was, like, I thought Mum would, m– I didn't really know how Mum would react because I never actually told her something like this before. And she said, 'Ierum, um, when you get home, I'm gonna, um, make you s– um, some vegetables for you to eat.' And, so then she started supporting me, sh-she made me look up, um, on my tablet for, like, workout videos and stuff, so I can do at home. And I done that on, um, Monday and Tuesday, Tuesday is when I noticed that my skirt got a bit loose, so I was really happy about my results. (*Laughs*.)

Ummm I'm doing History, because History is easier than Geography. I'm I'm I'm really not sure about all of this. I never actually thought what I want to do in the future. I want to get a lot of money yeah so I can get myself a house and –

LILY. – And a husband.

IERUM. Yeah but you can't buy a husband. You can't buy a husband. But like what subjects do I really need to work hard on to get a lot of money?

2.3.24. Best student

AYESHA *and* ALI*'s home*.

AYESHA. I got into Triple Science, I get more GCSEs so it's more wicked. I'm in Year 9. Ummm started doing my GCSEs and thingies and stuff, so hard. I don't know, before-I used to find Science really really boring, I used to just literally go sleep in his lessons but now I'm like a top top top I-I wanna get really high in my SAT– , in my GCSEs. Somehow I don't know makes so surprising I got best student. I was so shocked!

TASMIN. You know what it is I think what's kicked it off more is the fact that Ali's GCSEs and she sees how it's reflecting on Ali. Now he has to kind of stay a year back.

AYESHA. Me I wanna become a doctor. Chta. I just want to get out of school.

TASMIN. That's what you said this morning yesterday it was a PE teacher.

AYESHA. No. I don't.

TASMIN. She changes every single day.

2.3.25. An idolising

LUCAS*'s Philosophy lesson*.

MISS BURROWS. Lucas sorry you were gonna say, something about your family.

LUCAS. Er I was just saying my brothers as well.

MISS BURROWS. Mmmm.

LUCAS. Throughout your life, well my life I've had people coming up to me and saying, 'oh how's your brother doing in this amazing part of his life'.

MISS BURROWS. Umm –

LUCAS. An' you're like 'oh yeah, they're okay, they're doing, they're doing fine thanks' – (*Laughs*.)

MISS BURROWS. How am I?! / Are you not interested in me?

Laughter.

LUCAS. Ah. It gets me sooo angry. Er but yeah so you've gotta have them, you've gotta have them in your life because of that I mean / and because of that you aspire to be like them.

MISS BURROWS. Yeah.

Yeah definitely.

2.3.26. We drank tea

IERUM. So I've been umm bonding a lot of Lily lately. I went over to hers umm three weeks ago and I was pretty nervous and stuff cos she had like an older brother and umm her-her mum was there as well I had to like, I tried like to present myself sensibly. I continued keeping a happy smile on my face. I had tea with them, uhm as in like, like actual tea. I mean like we drank tea. I was pretty surprised when she told me that like every day like their family have tea and stuff like they all just drink tea. I'm like wow that's like a really nice posh family. I felt like really posh too.

2.3.27. Pressure to conform

LUCAS's *Philosophy lesson.*

MISS BURROWS. When you're young you're particularly impressionable and you start adopting the authorities that are around you and particularly from that age your main authority is your parents right? (*Beat.*) What about your age, who are your authorities?

SIOBHAN. Your peers.

MISS BURROWS. Good. I completely agree but why would you say your peers become an authority?

SIOBHAN. Pressure.

MISS BURROWS. Umm umm.

SIOBHAN. To conform.

MISS BURROWS. Okay.

LUCAS. All the amount of time you spend with them, / that's –

MISS BURROWS. Good. There's two things that you've mentioned there. Time spent and a pressure to conform which comes from somewhere. Okay that comes from some sort of ah feeling like you ought to be doing what everybody else is doing. Very normal.

2.3.28. Trees everywhere

A secluded farm cottage in the Kent countryside. A dog barks.

LUAN (*lethargically*). I'm with Joanna my host, like this is the host family I stay with when I'm here and that's about it. I just come here while, while I'm at Rochester and that's about it yeah. This is where I stay – during the week and that's about it yeah. Nothing much, just same old, that's it. Nothing different. It's umm very quiet and it's not really, there's not really that much you can do.

More barking.

That's about it. An' home's home innit, you've seen the difference like – bloody jus' trees everywhere. So yeah I just come here, eat, do some work, sleep and that's it, day done, just fields and that's it. Nothing else, nothing really. Yeah that's about it.

2.3.29. Focus on my work

CALLUM*'s form class.*

CALLUM. I don't want, I don't like saying it but unfortunately my form class is full of people who you know don't work the hardest and they kinda you know mess about so that was a bit of a shame cos I-I wanted to try and get away from all that. The main thing is the work, t' focus on my work. I just don't want to be disrupted in that. You know that's a main thing I want to get on with what I'm there to do an' that's to learn and get good results.

AIDEN. Margaret Thatcher.

CALLUM. Margaret Thatcher.

PUPILS *laugh*.

AIDEN. Well / done.

CALLUM. Best Prime Minister ever. Ruled with an iron fist. / She did what she had to do.

AIDEN. Oh my god.

CALLUM. Good woman. People always say oh Margaret Thatcher was a, you know the Iron Age it was, it was bad, like, ruled with an iron fist, you didn't get away with anything. That's good, look at us now! You know what I mean? It's all confusion. But I have no doubt that if that woman was here today and she was still Prime Minister, an'I, she wouldn't have taken any nonsense from the EU.

2.3.30. Went to the next level

LUCUS*'s bedroom suite at school*.

LUCAS (*beat*). I got busted for smoking. So ten-pound fine and, and gating for the weekend. Err you have to stay in house all weekend, you can't go out but it's just a weekend.

BEN *bursts in*.

BEN. Yes I knew it!

LUCAS *laughs*.

I wanted to come and see you because I don't know if Lucas will tell you.

LUCAS. About what?

BEN (*beat*). You and Georgie.

LUCAS *laughs*.

I just thought I'd tell, / tell you know, you just need to know.

LUCAS. Classic. What? No, no we're still on. Don't worry about it. Don't worry about it. It went to the next level.

BEN. They had sex.

They both laugh.

LUCAS. Ben, I was going to tell you, it would have come out, just burst through the doors.

BEN. I was ha', I was having a shower and I was like I've got to go and tell her.

LUCAS *laughs*.

LUCAS. Thanks, Ben. Hahahah. Umm oh when was it Ben? Three, three weeks a' –

BEN. 'Bout three weeks ago.

LUCAS. Three weeks ago. / Quite recent.

BEN *claps four times*.

Nah, back at afternoon te– ar-afternoon lunch at the fam house, at the house, at home. Ha ha. It was like tea. It was like after lunch she just came back for tea like it was like, 'oh Mum we're just gonna go chill upstairs'. Haha. She's like, 'cool'. – haha.

BEN. Be safe. / Ahuh. Risk it for a chocolate biscuit.

LUCAS. Yeah.

LUCAS *laughs*.

2.3.31. Big bust-up

LUAN*'s home*.

AGRON. He had a big bust-up with a girl over there.

LUAN. No it wasn't that, it wasn't that.

AGRON. He had a big bust-up with a girl.

LUAN. It wasn't that! What you on about?

AGRON. Yeah but we just going on to it you know, and there was a clash of personalities.

DRIN. What happened?

LUAN. Tah. She was crying cos we were just talking yeah about our age like she was like, 'ah I'm seventeen'. Cos I thought she was eighteen. She was like, 'ah I'm seventeen as well like', 'Oh really?!' and like I looked at 'em guys, I started laughing, I was like, 'ah I didn't know you were my age and stuff like that' and she started getting upset. She's like, 'I'm still older than you, I'm still older than you'. She started cryin'.

DRIN. So basically, you tried to move to a girl –

LUAN. I didn't move to her.

DRIN. – You tried to flirt and it backfired.

LUAN. I swear to god I didn't.

DRIN. Wow. / Imagine that, / you go to flirt with a girl and she starts crying! /

AGRON. 'Take your hands off him man.'

LULJETA. She, she wanted? –

No, no!

AGRON. Well why don't you teach him some moves then? / Why don't you teach him some –

LUAN. That wasn't it I didn't try to flirt with her / oh my days! She's annoying. She just / shouts all the time.

DRIN. I'm surprised.

LULJETA. Oh now I / understand. Oh poor thing. Ohhh. Poor thing. Thanks!

DRIN. I'm surprised.

Do you get it? He must have, he must have like, she must have thought, she must have thought, 'oh a boy from South London, ooooh where's my phone'.

AGRON. So end of the line he's gonna finish this year and then come to London.

LUAN. Yes.

AGRON. Yes.

LUAN. Just don't tell coach.

AGRON. So that's the story in Balamory.

2.3.32. Mascara

MIA *arrives at school with her eye make-up all smudged.*

MIA. My life's a joke at the minute. My life is just a joke.
I have'n ev'n been to college. (*Beat.*) This the first time I've
rocked up since (*Beat.*) November. It's five past one yeah
and I was meant to be in college at ten past nine this
morning.

   MIA *enters* MONNA*'s* (*her tutor's*) *classroom.*

I haven't got any assessments that need doin'.

MONNA. You got Plaitin' Twisting, that's what Cerys's doing
today. (*Beat.*) You got black all over your face.

MIA. I know.

MONNA. As if you've been crying. Your mascara's run down
your face.

   You bin cryin'?

MIA. No, I'm alright.

MONNA. What's all this then?

MIA. Oh I dunno. It's-just my make-up, it just hasn't gone
right.

MONNA. NO it's black as if it's tears darling. (*Beat.*) Go and
check yourself darl'. We'll see yer down there yeah?

   MIA *exits.*

   She has been cryin'.

2.3.33. Kickin' Chicken

ROBYN. She's had a bit of a day! Coz I've got a job now. I've
    got a job! Ah! It's at, I'm not joking it's at this place called
    Kickin' Chicken oh god! Okay it's a fast-food restaurant
    right, it's fucking disgusting. It's a fast-food restaurant, it's a
    bit like KFC but it's halal. An' they're fine, they're nice.
    I feel like my pores are constantly clogged with oil and I hate
    it, but I get sixty pounds a week, so it can't be that bad.
    Umm I've put it in my skull piggy bank and take it out when
    I need it. It's because I've got a job like I can't really go out
    on weekends but I can go out on Friday nights. We go to
    Well Street Pub. And they don't ID you so I'm like, love it.
    Oh yeah! No I like waddle in there with a full face make-up
    and I'm like, 'Rum and Coke please' and they're like –
    (*Mimes the barman serving her a drink. Beat.*) Is it okay if
    I roll a cigarette? Like I do not intend, like I'm, like I'm fully
    not intending to take this up much longer, but I've only
    properly been smoking like smoking-smoking for a year.

She tries and fails numerous times to light her cigarette.

2.3.34. Psycho ex-boyfriend

MIA*'s school loos.*

MIA *gets a text from her ex.*

MIA. Just leave me alone.

CADI. How old's he?

JODI. Twenny-two

CADI. Fucking 'ell.

MIA. I've got a psycho ex-boyfriend.

JODI. She split up with him today, yeah.

MIA (*emotional*). An' like he won't stop messaging me. 'Hope
    this lad was worth it Mia.' I'm not going with any other
    boys. I just wanna be on my own. I just wanna go back to
    bed and I just wanna cry, like I do every single fuckin' night.
    (*She sniffs.*) Cadi how long have you known me-when have
    you ever seen me like this. (*Sobbing. She throws up.*)

CADI. Right, I can get Monna.

MIA. No Cadi no!

CADI. Mia you gotta calm down okay, you're making yourself
ill. You gotta calm down, now.

MIA. Please don't get Monna. I won't speak to Monna, Cadi
I mean it, I won't speak to her. I'm not depressed, I'm not
deluded, an' everyone thinks I am! (*Weeps.*)

MONNA *enters*.

MONNA. Mia what's the problem?

MIA. Nothin'.

MONNA. So what's wrong with you?

MIA. Nothin', I'm I'm alright, I've just gotta go back to the
doctor's to get my tablets. Once I've back on my tablets, I'll
be okay.

MONNA. You've got an issue with this boyfriend haven't you?

MIA. Monna, he was sat there this morning while I was trying
to get ready and he was like, 'No lad would ever want you,
look at you.' An' he'll just keep messaging me and
messaging me. And he's telling me that he's got some girl
called Sara to come an' give me a hidin' after school, after
college-I'd –

MONNA. I think-I think you need to go home. Eh – I think you
need to go to the police, ya know, about this.

MIA s*ighs*.

2.3.35. Green eyes

TAYLOR*'s home*. TAYLOR *shows off his tattoos*.

PATRICIA. Tell her then.

TAYLOR. Yeah I got it done on holiday. / A tattoo, in America.

PATRICIA. In where?

What's it represent?

TAYLOR. What was it I can't remember?

PATRICIA. The first one was the lion.

TAYLOR. Yeah.

PATRICIA. The tiger-lion in you because –

TAYLOR. – Yeah cos I'm an aggressive little person when I need to be and then it's got / green eyes coz of Leena. It's a lion.

PATRICIA. Why the eyes.

   Why d'you-what's the green eyes?

TAYLOR. Cos of Leena she's got green eyes I did it to make her happy you see. Good boy I am yeah.

PATRICIA. It's a good time right now, but it's not really a good time right now because she's going through family troubles at home and he's such a support to her and it's cute.

GEORGE. Yeah he's been missing the gym so he can spend time with Leena and all sorts bless him.

2.3.36. I'm gonna rip her to pieces

MIA *shows the messages on her phone.*

MIA. This is it. Snapchat look. Telling me that that Sara wants to give me a hidin' are you daft? She's around fucking three foot tall and fucking fat I'd kick her everywhere. Sara Griffiths, I'm gonna kill her. (*Spits.*) I'm gonna rip her to pieces. I'm gonna hurt her. Watch what happens when I see that stupid little slag, I'm gonna hurt her.

   MIA*'s phone rings.*

   My head won't be fucked and I won't be suicidal if I had no phone. This is why I hate having a phone.

   MIA *answers and puts it on speakerphone. Her voice is brimming with emotion.*

   (*Inhales deeply.*) You have got fuck-all chances left now. Look at the way you speak to me.

EX-BOYFRIEND (*on speakerphone*). I'll / I'll, I'll –

MIA. You told me, yeah, that you'd kill any lad that ever hurt me, yeah, but look how much you've hurt me.

EX-BOYFRIEND (*on speakerphone*). I've not hurt / you're – ah –

MIA. You're doing to me, yeah, what my dad does to my mum! (*Cries.*)

EX-BOYFRIEND (*on speakerphone*). How am I?

MIA. You are nasty and spiteful. And you expect me to roll over and take it. I'm not gonna take it any more!

EX-BOYFRIEND (*on speakerphone*). Well, I can't stop if you're just saying you're leaving me / now, d'you know what I mean?

MIA *spits*.

(*Sighs.*) So, what, you weren't planning on seeing me tonight now?

MIA. I-I.

EX-BOYFRIEND (*on speakerphone*). What?

MIA. I gotta go, I got a meeting.

EX-BOYFRIEND (*on speakerphone*). Yeah, your boys are coming – / (*Mumbles.*)

MIA. No! I've got a meeting in college.

EX-BOYFRIEND (*on speakerphone*). What meeting?

MIA. I don't know, with some welfare officer.

EX-BOYFRIEND (*on speakerphone*). Oh yeah?

MIA. Yeah!

EX-BOYFRIEND (*on speakerphone*). Yeah, alright then.

MIA. Whatever. See? I can't even go to a fucking meeting. Ladies and gentleman? That's Mia's fucking baby daddy. (*Spits.*)

2.3.37. School prefect

LUCAS. This is the time of the year where people er get chosen for prefects and stuff. Well hopefully I get at least a prefect.

EMILY. I applied for Head of House by writing a letter, I wrote it ages ago, and now they've narrowed it down to like four people.

LUCAS. Three boys and three girls get interviewed.

EMILY. Four girls and three boys.

LUCAS. I'll probably get interviewed.

EMILY. So there's one Head of House in each house and then in each house there's also typically one school prefect.

LUCAS. N-never to my knowledge at Elland has there been two brothers in consecutive years as Head of Schools.

EMILY. Head of House or school prefect would be nice.

LUCAS. I'm probably not the best candidate for it. I mean people think I am but you've gotta be good at everything and you've gotta be so on it and dedicated and you can't break a single rule and I just don't want that stress on me.

EMILY. They'll just decide who they want it to be I guess, I don't know.

2.3.38. Complete cleanse

LUCAS. I've also deleted all my Snapchat, Facebook, Instagram, Facebook Messenger. It's so nice, erm just complete cleanse.

2.3.39. I got a new phone

IERUM. 'Wooo' I've got a new phone! Hooray, yeahhh! (*Laughs.*) Yeah! (*Laughs.*) I'm not really like obsessed with it. Um hm, I was really happy when it happened. I downloaded Instagram and umm ahh Sienna was really supportive, like so she was jus' like, 'ohhhh' she sent lots of messages to everyone saying, 'Oh Ierum's has a new

Instagram account go follow her, go message her and stuff.
That it's Ierum, whoa!!!' And I was really happy. (*Beat.*)
I get to actually see what's going on and then so I don't feel
left out any more.

2.3.40. I can't stop being sick

MIA. I can't, stop, being, sick. I've put weight on, I can't stop
being sick, er, I've, like, it hurts (*Beat.*) like, my stomach
hurts, like, I can feel it swelling, it's horrible. I can't eat,
I can't keep anything down. Like, the smell of food makes
me feel sick. (*Pause.*) What if I'm pregnant? What if I'm
not? What if I'm pregnant?

2.3.41. Drive-by shooting

A hospital ward. Birmingham. ALI, AYESHA *and* TASMIN
stand beside Uzma's hospital bed.

ALI. My mum took Uzma to Pakistan on a holiday, Uzma is my
little sister. They got basically caught up in a drive-by
shooting. So, we don't know who's done it like if there's
(*Beat.*) any links to why this has been done no one knows
yet. So my little sister she was sitting in the front seat and
my dad's brother sitting in the front seat holding the baby
because in Pakistan they do that. And my mum's sitting in
the back, a motorbike's come with a guy with a gun, comes
to the side of the car and they've shhh, like fired several
times. So, a bullet's gone through my uncle's arm, ah a
bullet's gone through Uzma's tummy, her arm and her hand.
Yeah and she was in so much pain. I've got photos, do you
want to see? They're really upsetting. She's four.

Beat.

AYESHA. I had, I had an exam and I literally (*Beat.*) it's
probably one of the most my end-of-year target's exams.
Yeah and I, I pro– I failed all of them I can tell you.
Yesterday I stayed the whole day off school and spent it with
Uzma. And she was actually so happy and then this morning
miss was like, 'oh you've taken another day off' and 'oh if

you want to go visit your sister then you have to visit her out of school', and you know, I was just dead out of the conversation.

TASMIN. I'm gonna wake up and it's all like this really really bad dream. Innit poppet? (*Beat.*) No. (*Beat.*)

Do you know you don't know if your kid's going to make it through the night or – (*Pause.*)

ALI. It's like do you know when you're walking alone in the street in the night and your phone battery dies and you don't know what to do. That's like this situation, / when you're lost that's what it was like.

AYESHA. It – I – (*Beat.*) I, I was speechless.

TASMIN. What a nice way to describe it.

She laughs gently.

ALI. Literally, all your mobile data finishes.

They all laugh.

TASMIN. I love you too son.

The hospital equipment beeps unexpectedly.

Oh come on.

They look round anxiously for the nurse but she doesn't come.

ACT FOUR

2.4.1. A reading

LUCAS*'s school chapel.*

The school choir sings 'Cantate Domino' by Giuseppe Pitoni.
LUCAS *walks down the aisle to the lectern.*

LUCAS. A reading from the Gospel of Saint Luke.

2.4.2. Creative Arts

ROBYN. I've applied for college umm – it opened up on
    sixteenth I applied for college. Umm I applied for (*Coughs.*)
    two courses. Umm Creative Arts, TV Drama and Creative
    Arts, Film and Screenwriting. I wanna like create stories and
    tell them an' like – since I was like a kid like it's always been
    my thing.

2.4.3. Shitting myself

Outside chapel.

REVEREND STUART ROBERTSON. You were very assured.

LUCAS. Thank you, that's appreciate-cheers.

REVEREND STUART ROBERTSON. Ahm, you know, I
    sensed you were a bit nervous in the vestry beforehand.

LUCAS (*laughs*). Yeah.

REVEREND STUART ROBERTSON. But actually when it
    came to the crunch time you were absolutely spot-on.

LUCAS. Thank you very much.

REVEREND STUART ROBERTSON. Yeah well done. Stuart
    Robertson, nice to meet you.

REVEREND STUART ROBERTSON *exits*.

LUCAS. I was shitting myself.

2.4.4. Blew away my interview

LUCAS. I got Head of School and I was kind of like why?!
(*Laughs*.) Umm but apparently I just blew away my
interview. They – I practised a bit of what to say (*Beat*.) with
– with Ted, which is always helpful having ya (*Beat*.) brother
as Head Boy as well. Umm that's another weird thing. First
time in five hundred years that's ever happened. (*Pause*.)
Yeah it's just a lot of work, there's so much I've got to do.
And with A levels and everything and cos I'm not naturally
the most intelligent person, it's gonna be flippin' difficult.

2.4.5. Mrs Griffin's office

EMILY*'s home*.

EMILY. Oh they they emailed me and they're like, 'oh you need
to come in for a tutorial'. So that was my tutor so I went into
my tutor's office in the morning and he was like, 'We're
gonna continue your tutorial in Mrs Griffin's office and
I was like, 'right okay then'.

JEN. Thinking, 'Ooooh, / who's a naughty girl!'

EMILY. So, so they lead me to Mrs Griffin's office and they're
like, 'do you know why you're here?' and I was like, 'I hope
so because I haven't done anything wrong'. / And they were
like, / they were like, 'Umm would you like to be Head of
House?' and I was like, 'yes, thank you very much'. / Yeah.
That was pretty much it.

JEN. Ha ha.

Nothing you haven't found out about!

JEN *laughs*.

2.4.6. Excellent start

LUAN*'s new school near Worcester.*

MR SULLIVAN. He's settling in really well. I mean he's been, we've – we've got house captains and he's been put forward as one of the house captains. Umm / and so coz he's really – he's doing really well and he's nominated by the basketballers. An' but and so yes it's made – made an excellent start. We have a basketball academy yes and linked with Worcester Wolves erm and he, and it's very selective. Erm hence, he's come up here and boarding and then doing lots of basketball from about six-thirty in the morning to six-thirty at night isn't it with lessons in, / in there as well.

LUAN. Yeah.

Oh yeah.

Thank you, sir. (*Beat.*) Like the academy itself, I'd say well to be fair we're pretty much like number-one team in the country. Yeah. Yeah I'm happy now, I'm not naughty.

2.4.7. Greg from *Love Island*

EMILY*'s school noticeboard.* PUPILS *gather round.*

EMILY. So I've had to do the duty rotas which is quite basic (*Beat.*) well no um I say that, but it takes so long. (*Beat.*) Ah yes timetables. It's the first year back – first day back sorry. This is my timetable. So I've got RS next. Guys is lunch after period four or period five?

OSCAR. Period four.

PIP. Period four.

EMILY. Right okay. Also, Luella have you seen the new rugby coach he looks like, Luella the new rugby coach looks like Greg from *Love Island*, you're not on the group chat so you didn't see the picture but he looks like Greg from *Love* –

LUELLA. What's his name? –

EMILY. – Come here. (*Beat.*) I don't know what his name is. But look he looks like / Greg from *Love Island*.

LUELLA. Oh my god, if he be my coach I'm gonna be happy.

EMILY. Greg Wallum. Oh, where's the picture?

SASHA. What did he send it to you on?

EMILY *searches on her phone.*

EMILY. You know. I-I posted it on my phone cos I was like 'everybody look' – (*Laughs.*)

LUELLA. This better be good Ems.

EMILY. No it is. He looks just, he looks just like him.

EMILY *shows the photo.*

LUELLA. Fair.

EMILY. Yeah he does.

LUELLA. He better be my coach.

2.4.8. Given up on school

ALI *and* AYESHA*'s home.*

AYESHA. Ah I've had the shittiest day at school… I had an argument with all of my teachers. You know this Uzma thing-innit – Uh I've given up on school.

ALI. College is getting really annoying now because I have like so much work to give in and everythink and because now this whole thing has happened I haven't had time to literally apply for anything because I'm so just like – my routine is just college, wake up, get ready, college, come home, no go hospital, come back home, get into bed, I'd be shattered. Watch *Prison Break* for like (*Beat.*) two episodes and then just fall asleep. (*Beat.*) Basically my little sister, she came out from the hospital like two weeks ago. Like everything was fine but like a few days ago she started to limp and there was a piece of erm co– you know like cotton wool left over from Pakistan, like I think it was part of a bandage – stuck inside of her – (*Beat.*) wound and it was coming out. Obviously it was serious so… Yesterday we took her to children's – the emergency department. It's a day's surgery so hopefully she'll – they'll let her home.

AYESHA. Uhh. It's literally turned my whole family around.

ALI. Like I feel like Ayesha's taking a role on the house and I've taken a role on obviously being more with now with her.

AYESHA. We got a new washing machine, I learned how to do that. I wasn't planning on to ever learn how to do that cos I hate doing the washing machine. (*Beat.*) I can't wait when we go back in our house, an' she's normal. She comes to my room / an' she jumps on my bed and I go, 'Uzma go away!' Like before she was leaving to Pakistan we were like, 'Yay, no more / Uzma coming to our room'.

ALI. Haha.

I know! I was so glad, I was so glad.

They giggle.

Now I / was like – if I could rewind time I would.

AYESHA. Now I'm like, 'Uzma come to my room'.

2.4.9. Out our head

ROBYN. I feel really lost. I live in a council flat, I'm going to college, I almost got kicked out of school, I work in a fast-food restaurant! This is like a Channel 4 after-school special! I'm like a troubled teen. Dad's been getting sicker. Mum's getting more stressed. Eh, best friend's still housebound with depression, anxiety – bad acid. Everyone my age takes a shit-ton of drugs. But yeah, I don't know, you forget, huh-huh this is Glasgow – ha, there's like fifteen-year-olds doing diazepam. Haa. Like what I've seen we're all fuckin' out er head, cos it's like we grew up where it was like the kind of change with technology. We're all kind of mentally ill ha, and we don't sleep enough.

2.4.10. Betrayed

IERUM*'s home.*

IERUM. Sienna brought up that Francheska was having like erm
– a party. So then umm I'm like, 'really?' like, 'when is it?',
like, 'what's the details an' stuff?' and she's like, 'oh she didn't
decide yet', and everything and umm this week on Friday I
saw Sienna, Lily, umm'nd Marni, Eliza and Cassie they're all
like in a circle and they're all like talking about umm like
what they're gonna wear and stuff. And so then I'm thinking,
oh they're talking about Halloween (*Beat.*) ta but umm, umm
when I went home (*Beat.*) like on my phone I saw like umm –
(*Beat.*) umm videos and like pictures of like a party of umm
everyone in a party an' stuff and then that's when I realised it
was Francheska's party. I had missed it. I was just oh. So and
I, I don't – in a way I kind of like felt like I was betrayed and
like – it looked really really fun. Umm Josh was the DJ, Josh
actually went there. (*Beat.*) I mean it just really u– made me
upset (*She starts to cry.*) like the whole party thing. It made
me upset. An' I was really looking forward to like going out
umm in this, in these fourth – in these three weeks. Cos like
these are like the only three weeks that I can actually go out
and stuff in the entire year. Just because my dad left to go like
to his country. It's fine.

2.4.11. Eyelids were swelling up

CALLUM*'s home.*

CALLUM. My face had been bad a lot last year in school. An'
it had always been quite red and then we went away on
holiday. And it just went whoaf! So, we went to the, the
hospital. (*Beat.*) Hmm hmm. In Lagos, Portugal – and I had
like a (*Beat.*) a drip in me and got bloods taken and that
seemed to settle it for a bit. On the flight back I'd been
scratching – in a lot / of pain. It was –

MARGARET. His face was starting to get really tight, he
couldn't move his mouth.

CALLUM. And my face's getting all inflamed and like all
bubbly. I was like, 'jeepers' my eyelids were swelling up.

And eventually we-we got back and ah throughout the night I got up every, I don't know, half an hour to an hour and put my medicated cream on it, thinking on it would make it better, and I woke up in the morning I couldn't see.

MARGARET. Couldn't open his eyes. I just thought, what is this? Since that happened he just – didn't want to leave the house. Just didn't want to go anywhere, do anything cos 'is – he just felt people were staring at him all the time you know.

RONALD. Told you, t' get 'im a wee bell.

CALLUM. L-like the – the – the guy the private dermatologist has said the first thing we'd probably go to is like light treatment, and after that they said if that doesn't work they'd probably have to go to –

RONALD. Drugs –

CALLUM. – Methotrexate.

RONALD. – Methotrexate which is – I-I was on methotrexate.

CALLUM. S'like a form of chemotherapy it wrecks your immune system / eventually.

RONALD. Yeah. But stress can be a, then she was, she was saying like, 'are you stressed about stuff?' / Obviously you're going through the difficult age, an' it's exams and all sorts of things. When's your GCSEs then?

CALLUM. Well.

My GCSEs are in, they're in the same as last year June. But this time, instead of three or four single exams I'll have about (*Beat.*) twenty-five.

2.4.12. Eczema

ZAC*'s home.*

NAJMA. We went, we went to the doctor and we said you know, er they literally looked at it, he goes, 'er an' that's eczema, that's usually caused by stress'. And Zac / goes 'I'm not stressed' an' I go. And I kind of said – / we talked about it but I kind of said he's not stressed but his body is /going –

ZAC. An' I was like –

Something like –

My, my body is clearly stressed.

NAJMA. Hair falling out, eczema round your eyelids. (*Beat*.) Yeah / it's all going on.

ZAC. It's deep.

Laughter.

2.4.13. I didn't pass

EMILY*'s home*.

EMILY. No. (*Beat*.) I didn't pass.

JEN. Failed her test, driving test.

EMILY. Hmmm yeah I know. It's fine. (*Beat*.) Argh. Yeah I'm not gonna try again though, I don't really want to. Argh. I'm so tired, yeah it just been a really really long week I've have like eight million things going on. (*Coughing*.) Hmmm. I've got an awful cough as well. (*Beat*.) Uh so I applied to York, Birmingham, Bristol, Newcastle. (*Beat*.) Oh my god. Right I need to go work I'm sorry. I have so much stuff to do. I don't want to. Argh!!!! (*Coughing*.)

JEN. My poor little girlie girl.

2.4.14. My life is going quiet good

ALI. Kim Kardashian had a baby. And thingy, the royal family had a baby as well. That's – (*Beat*.) nn– nice. Meghan Markle's American. I bet they were so gassed the Americans. The baby – is the baby going to be a quarter black then? That's so cool. Hopefully a Pakistani person will make it. (*Beat*.) College I'm loving it. The new friends that I've just made – amazing! Co– the work is kind of tricky but otherwise an' that, my life is going (*Beat*.) quiet good at the moment. I'm l' – absolutely love working you know. It's so lovely. Playtime – you know the toy shop? And the pay – an' the pay is really good as well. Seven pounds seventy an hour.

(*Beat.*) Oh clothes – I bought thi' jacket yesterday. Yeah in Forever 21 and they were closing down for seven pounds. I worked – I served a customer for this jacket.

ALI *laughs*.

2.4.15. The Engels Society Environmental Manifesto

LUCAS*'s school common room.*

LUCAS. We have a manifesto. The Engels Society Environmental Manifesto which like outlines what we wish the school to do – yeah. There's about seven of us. It's quite small. Er, I bring my coffee machine in sometimes, have coffees, it's just very chilled out. So. It's nice. (*Beat.*) I dunno, I jus' – jus' quite like the idea of a more equal society, cos I just get annoyed at Ell–, like at the general system that's happening at the moment.

2.4.16. Name on the map

LUAN. I got called up for the Euros, so the Kosovan national team, you probably heard that we won it and everything? Which was pretty good yeah. It was actually sick. All my like, my paren', like all my relatives like family came to watch the first game, so my grandad and everything. After that game literally everyone looked at me like, 'Who's this guy?' The Kosovan Federation people like big names talking about my name. 'You see that number-thirteen kid whoa he's good, he's really good.' You hear my name everywhere, everyone's just talking about me, everyone's excited about me. Like we're all, we're all live on TV when all these games were going on. Like everyone's watching us live on TV. I was like, so many – oh if I had my phone, my phone actually got confiscated, but if I had my phone I'd show you. But, ha. It's the first time we've gone to a finals, Kosovo has gone to a finals, everyone's so excited. And like it's history made, everyone's going crazy. Yeah my dad, my dad, my dad was so proud I could just see, he was so proud. All my family members were like, I put my name, our na– our family name on the map.

2.4.17. The year of Robyn

ROBYN. Uhm, college is great, I'm having so much fun. I'm in
two and a half days a week. I'm getting SAAS which is like
student loans but like in S– I don't know if it's different
down in England but in Scotland you only pay back your
student loans if you like, make enough money to. (*Beat*.)
Yeah. (*Beat*.) Parent income establishes how much you get.
I'm eligible for a lot of fucking money because my parents –
(*Beat*.) are underpaid. I don't feel as lost any more which is
quite nice. It's the year of Robyn but technically in my life
every year is the year of Robyn.

2.4.18. They went Soho

LUAN*'s home. The table is laid with the tablecloth and there's
a bowl of hummus with carrots. It's lunchtime and* LUAN *is still
in bed*.

LULJETA. We don't know exactly what time he came back, but
he was asleep when I / looked last time.

AGRON. They went Soho.

LULJETA. He doesn't know, he's just saying.

AGRON. He – they went Soho! Yeah man they had a blast.

LULJETA. We don't know where they went, they didn't tell us.

AGRON. We'll still very protective of them but now he has a
passport innit. Now that he's eighteen, open sesame innit.

LULJETA (*offering to the audience*). So help yourself, please.

AGRON (*to the audience*). Have some carrots, do you like
carrots? Get some hummus love. Did you know (*Beat*.) they
won? Claybrook College they won the ABL Trophy, the best
in the country. He got the medal. (*Clicks his cheek*.) My guy.
That's like the equivalent to Champions League.

LUAN *enters in his dressing gown*.

Hey Luan! Whoa there! Yeah! Leave the phone. So come
and sit here then.

LUAN. Nah I wanna sit here, I wanna sit here.

LUAN *sits on the sofa. Beat.*

AGRON. Oh my god, where've you been last night? You had a good time?

LUAN. Yeah.

AGRON. Where did you go London?

LUAN. No Chang's house.

AGRON. Oh you didn't go Soho?

LUAN. No.

AGRON. You didn't go Soho?

LUAN. We just played, we just played Xbox an' chilled.

AGRON. Did you drink last night?

LUAN. No.

AGRON. No alcohol?

LUAN. No, / this is not necessary.

AGRON. Oh yeah, he doesn't drink alcohol by the way. No.

LUAN. No we don't really drink that.

AGRON. Stand up, let's see how tall you are.

AGRON *playfully taps* LUAN *around the face and ruffles his hair.*

LUAN. Baba-why are you doing this. Just, chill out man argh. / I just woke up man, ahh just chill out. / Argh man.

AGRON. I'm chilled, I'm chilled.

I'm chilled man.

Beat. Cupping LUAN *round the face fondly.*

My Lu, my Lu, my Lu, man he-is so moody with me. Why?

LUAN. I just woke up Dad.

2.4.19. I'm a big-arsed softie

TAYLOR*'s home*.

TAYLOR. It's actually weird though yeah, like people our age managing to stay together. Cos / other boys are shagging about.

LEENA. I swear though everyone's like-like, 'oh my god you're so cute'.

TAYLOR. Ah yeah I think that –

LEENA. I'm not like twelve (*Beat*.) any more.

TAYLOR. People go, 'How long you've been together?' I go, 'four years'. Ah you're so cute.' It's not cute though. It's just (*Beat*.) you know what I mean?

LEENA. When, when we we're with people yeah he never like, he's not, he's like the hard lad yeah, / but then when he's just with me yeah / he's like this –

TAYLOR (*laughing*). Yeah cos I feel like – (*Beat*.)

Yeah I'm a big-arsed softie.

LEENA. – F'king little bear / yeah.

TAYLOR. Yeah, I wanna show you love but… it's…

LEENA. Aw. He FaceTimes me, I answer an' he started crying on FaceTime because I look pretty.

TAYLOR. I think that's happens like three times in four years.

LEENA. He started crying! (*Laughing*.)

TAYLOR. More – not not more than five times.

2.4.20. Do you have a girlfriend?

Same as 2.4.18.

AGRON. Do you have a girlfriend Luan?

LUAN. No.

   Pause.

AGRON. You don't have a girlfriend?

Beat.

LULJETA. He's too busy with basketball, don't have time to have a girlfriend. He's clever boy.

Pause.

AGRON. Why not Lu?

LUAN. Cos I don't want one Dad.

AGRON. Why?

LUAN. What's the point, I can't really be bothered can I.

AGRON. What do you mean can't be bothered?

LUAN. It's bit long is it.

AGRON. What?

LUAN. It's a bit long.

AGRON. What do you mean long?

LUAN. It's a bit long Dad. Like it's too much effort, it's a bit long, can't be bothered.

LULJETA. It's too young to have a girlfriend. / Plenty – plenty –

AGRON. 'Scuse me, he's nineteen.

LULJETA. Plenty of time.

Pause.

AGRON. I think he should have a girlfriend man.

Beat.

LUAN. Ha, ha. Nah.

AGRON. It will settle his nerves down a bit you know, you know. Luljeta, I'm gonna have to go. Do you have a girlfriend Lu?

LUAN. No!

AGRON. I'm going then before he gets mad at me. Ciao!

AGRON *leaves.*

2.4.21. I'm shocked

A café.

ANNABELLA. I started talking to Toby. Who's my new
boyfriend. Umm Toby put up on his story, er, 'does any, does
anyone want to spit half a yoke?' A yoke, like Ec-Ecstasy –
and my friend, Anna sent it to me and she was like, 'oh my
god Bella like please like can you get this for me, I don't
like'. Cos, she – she goes to school with Toby and it would
be awkward and then umm he's like, 'oh look I think you
should be my girlfriend'. and I was like, 'no way!' like, 'me
too'. He's so lovely, like he is so nice to me, like anything I
say like he's like, 'yeah perfect like whatever you want'.
Like I could be like, 'oh trees, like I like trees', and he'd be
like, 'ah trees are so good you're so right, Bella like trees are
amazing'. (*Beat.*) I'm actually I was meant to meet up with
him, I'll text him and ah.

She reads a message on her phone.

Oh my god. (*Beat.*) Mum.

ALBERTA *enters.*

Toby's just text me. He's ended it with me.

ALBERTA. What!

ANNABELLA. Yeah. No don't touch my phone – (*Beat.*)

ALBERTA. Are you? (*Pause.*) What!

ANNABELLA. I'm shocked.

ALBERTA. I'm shocked.

ANNABELLA. Listen so ah – (*Reading out the text.*) 'okay,
I'm really sorry for this but you said you wanted me to be
honest and I – I really think we should end this now. I just
don't want to be in a relationship right now, I want to focus
on my GCSEs for a bit and I'm sorry but like I hope – we –
can – stay – friends. I'm really sorry about doing this on
Snapchat by the way I just don't – think – I would've been
able to do it in person. (*Beat.*) Oh my god Mum.

ALBERTA. Oh darling, I'm so sorry. I'm so sorry for you.

ANNABELLA. No I'm not even like sad with it other than that, I'm just like shocked.

ALBERTA. I'm so sorry. I swear I thought like he was the one, didn't I?

ANNABELLA. I just, I can't, on Snapchat!

2.4.22. It's love

Glasgow city centre.

ROBYN (*unable to hold back her blushes*). This is, this is Rob. / Oh God! He's ma– (*Beat.*) boyfriend. Surprise!

ROB. Oh!

Hello. (*Beat*) We've been seeing each other for like –

ROBYN. Two months?

ROB. Yeah?

ROBYN. Coming up two months?

ROB. Coming up two –

ROBYN. There's no like – anniversary.

ROB. No well, there probably should do.

ROBYN. If we tracked back we could probably find it but –

ROB. I'm not trackin' back.

ROB *points at* ROBYN*'s love bite.*

It's – it's a hickey.

ROBYN. Yeah shut up.

ROB. A love bite some call er it on the neck.

ROBYN. It's on *my* neck.

ROB. I have, I have quite a lot on my shoulders. Gotta be honest. (*Beat.*) Do you want to see? (*Pause.*) Okay, okay.

ROBYN. We haven't been on a lot of dates.

ROB. Well.

ROBYN. Pizza Express does not count. I will reiterate this yet again.

ROB. We've been to McDonald's.

ROBYN. McDonald's doesn't count either. And neither does breakfast at Hot Doughnut.

ROB. Yeah we love each other. Yeah we've said it, love you. So it's, yeah it's love. So yeah, I'd, yeah, I'd say so.

ROB *laughs*.

2.4.23. Romance ensemble

Music plays. The youngsters mill around, as if at a school disco.

ROBYN. I don't wanna jump into things but I have very strong feelings for him.

IERUM. I didn't catch any feelings for like – any boys in my school.

ROBYN. Ahh, y' – I feel great. I really – (*Beat.*) yeah I love 'im. It's (*Beat.*) errr, ahh, it's a thing!

IERUM. I guess like cos like I don't really – think about that stuff. Cos I feel like I'm quite abnormal for not thinking that way.

ROBYN. I'm ahh – but like ohhhh. Oh he's great. Eeee, aaaarrr, aaah.

LUAN. I don't, I don't have a girl. Nah I just focus on my basketball and my studies.

AYESHA. I'm not falling in love because one I'm not allowed.

EMILY. No, no, absolutely not.

ZAC. No-for-it – It def, it definitely is love.

CALLUM. Oh of course yeah I mean I'm not, I'm not gonna be opposed to the idea but.

ZAC. I just literally felt my heart go like fffff – jus' close up.

AYESHA. Two, I can't be bothered to with it.

EMILY. I just can't be bothered with Tinder to be honest; it seems like a bit of effort.

AYESHA. Three, it never works out.

LUCAS. I ended it with Georgie.

ANNABELLA. I ju' just think boys these days are literally such (*Beat.*) dicks. Personally, I don't think there's anybody good enough for me.

LUCAS. But then I've got back with Georgie.

ALI. Cos like I wanna like save up some money for obviously like a wedding.

TAYLOR. I'm not having kids until my basketball career is like – gone to a finish.

CALLUM. If it happens it happens, it's not like, it's never been my priority. Education is the, the most important thing.

ALI. I can't believe we're talking about weddings? Innit? What the hell, what-what happened to me being in school?

2.4.24. Ten charges

MIA. I've just had a really really shit time yeah. (*Pause.*) Got into like really bad, like really really badly abusive relationship for thirteen and a half months. (*Beat.*) Do you remember when you come to see me last when we're in college? It's the same lad. He was on bail. So he's admitted, they he's admitted to one allegation which was throwing me round. They've got ten charges, then they've also now got charges for coercin' an' controlling behaviour. He'd ripped all my hair out, left big dents on my knees where he'd like jump on top of me and stuff, kicked me round the plot, smacked my head against the side, this is just in like one day yeah. (*Pause.*) I overdosed yeah. So I ended up workin' for my mum again so she could keep an eye on me. Started like seeing a new lad, but I don't want to say anything to my mum yet because I don't know how serious it is.

2.4.25. Child neglect

A café.

ALBERTA. Umm, I went down with Annabella on Thursday
and (*Beat.*) th-we took her into care. Umm, I need – I needed
it to happen. I don't know about Annabella but I definitely
needed it to happen it was, it wasn't fair on either of us. And
it is to support me. Since I took sepsis I haven't been (*Beat.*)
great on my housework. The house is (*Beat.*) horrendous,
horrendously untidy, messy, dirty at the minute. I mean it
really is it was – condition wise she shouldn't have to live
like that. It broke my heart. (*Beat.*) It's in her best interest
I wasn't coping. The wom'n – the social worker said that
I could be done for child neglect (*Beat.*) because umm
Annabella wasn't getting hot meals in the evening. Now she
was getting, she – you were, getting takeaway like.

ANNABELLA. Takeaway.

ALBERTA. Ah ha.

2.4.26. The cramps

ROBYN. I'm going on the pill so. It's er, something for my
horrific period cramps. So that's all fun. The idea of having
a kid isn't daunting, the idea of being pregnant is daunting.
You know what I mean. (*Beat.*) Fuck. No drinking for nine
months! I ain't ready for that shit. But it was either this or
having to deal with the cramps and er condoms are
incredibly expensive, three for five pounds in the Co-op.
I thought two birds with one stone you know.

2.4.27. Perfume

Same as 2.4.25.

ALBERTA. Part of the problem as well was that I got angry and
I fired up a bottle of perfume at her – up the stairs so that put
me down as 'violent'. It got to that point and I was just like –
(*Beat.*) I'm, I am going to hit her if I don't let her go. It was a
hard decision, hardest of my life actually to be honest.

ANNABELLA. Erm but like, I dunno I'm lot happier now, we both get on like way better.

ALBERTA. Yeah.

ANNABELLA. It's just like a big house.

ALBERTA. The children's home.

ANNABELLA. Umm everyone's been really nice to me. It's not as hard as everyone's making it out to be honestly.

ALBERTA. It is for me.

2.4.28. *Mock the Week*

ROBYN. Like my mum was like, my mum hinted – at – like we hadn't gotten to that stage yet and I looked at her and then she was like, 'oh baby'. and I was like 'euuugh'. I don't know, it's cool. (*Beat.*) One time – you know going at it – umm and I was like – I knew they were like downstairs so I was like – you know making him be quiet and shit, I paused for a second I was like, and I could hear them laughing downstairs and I knew for a fact *Mock the Week* was over, so it wasn't at that.

2.4.29. Stop talking

IERUM*'s English lesson. She holds her marked test.*

IERUM. Miss I'm not happy with my test. I'm not happy with my results.

MISS NOTLEY. I'm not happy with what you did Ierum. / So –

IERUM. Okay well, I've actually tried.

MISS NOTLEY. No you haven't, you / haven't.

IERUM. And you gave everyone else extra time in the classroom and literally William was on his là– Chromebook.

MISS NOTLEY. Ah Ierum, you sat there for most of / the lesson –

IERUM. Yeah / after lunchtime.

MISS NOTLEY. Stop talking / stop talking stop talking stop talking –

IERUM. After lunchtime when I was hot and I was tired.

MISS NOTLEY. – Stop talking.

IERUM. This is ridic/ulous.

MISS NOTLEY. Stop talking.

IERUM. I'm not accepting this. / This isn't, this isn't, this isn't my result. / I can do much more better than this. / I'm not accepting this.

MISS NOTLEY. That is your result...

That is your result.

Yes you can Ierum. You can!

IERUM. Exactly so why, so why won't you give me –

MISS NOTLEY. Outside, I want to have a conversation.

IERUM. I don't wanna. Ta. Oh my God-ah!

IERUM *exits followed by* MISS NOTLEY.

2.4.30. Wagged college

Oxford Street.

ALI. Can you believe we're actually like in London, oh my god. Shall we take a selfie? I feel like I'm in New York. They've come all the way to London to come to Primark. (*Beat.*) We're in, / ten of us, ten Sparkbrookie's in Londi.

COUSIN 2. Ten.

AYESHA. We're going put this all over Snapchat.

COUSIN 1. About what?

AYESHA. It's the full-on Snapchat entertainment.

ALI. No I don't like that one, let's take one round here. (*Camera click*) That came out so nice! Be obsessed with yourself because you never (*Beat.*) meet anyone like yourself.

AYESHA. That is the most dumbest quote I've ever met.

ALI. Well then don't listen to me.

2.4.31. Frustrated

The corridor outside IERUM*'s English class.*

MISS NOTLEY. Are you ready to come back in now Ierum? Because people are making improvements so this could be your opportunity to write something better – than you did last time?

IERUM. Well I don't want to be in this class any more. I made the / choice, I don't wanna be in this class.

MISS NOTLEY. It's not your choice, you are the student.

IERUM. Okay but that is not my score. / That is not my score.

MISS NOTLEY. That is your score Ierum.

IERUM. That's not my score, I don't get that's my score.

MISS NOTLEY. You're not taking responsibility for it unfortunately.

IERUM. Okay.

MISS NOTLEY. And I understand, I can see that you're frustrated, but you've got to be frustrated with yourself.

IERUM. I'm not frustrated with myself.

MISS NOTLEY. Then that is a problem.

IERUM. Okay fine.

MISS NOTLEY. Because I'm very frustrated with you.

IERUM. Okay that's fine.

2.4.32. Blast music and party

Oxford Street. Same as 2.4.30.

AYESHA. I should be in school right now. Forget education.
I took the day off.

ALI. Yeah I-I wagged college today. Yeah I couldn't be
bothered to go in.

AYESHA. I told my friends on my group chat at / school. To
tell 'em all my teachers that I'm ill. They probably told them
that I had that, you know that got that virus that's is going
round every school. My pr-iends probably told them I had
that. I've given up on school. I was in a mind I was like, 'do
I go to school to do my mock exam or do I come London?'

COUSIN 2 (*coughs*). You have mock exam today? What subject?

AYESHA. Maths.

COUSIN 2. Oh my god. Hahaha.

Music plays from their speaker.

COUSIN 1. That's Selfridges.

AYESHA. We've literally just bought a speaker to blast music
and party, because, why not? Hah.

AYESHA *and* COUSIN 1 *sing along to the music.*

ALI. We're not on the coach ya know.

AYESHA. I wanna dance, someone take a video of me.

2.4.33. Mastery

IERUM. Mr Thompson, good news. I might be coming to your
class soon.

MR THOMPSON. To my class?

IERUM. Yeah.

MR THOMPSON. Why has Miss Notley had enough?

IERUM. No just like, it f–, it's just like cos you're a really a good
English teacher and you're like getting me mastery so easily.

MR THOMPSON. No-ai-okay-I think you were getting yourself mastery by working hard weren't you?

Pause.

IERUM. Just giving you a heads-up.

2.4.34. Panda eyes

ZAC *walks around his bedroom checking for last items to pack.*

ZAC. One last chord (*He strikes the piano.*) on that piano. Go get the other key-keyboard you know, get last one on the Wurlitzer. (*He plays the Wurlitzer.*) Yah, that one there. Er what else? Eh yeah catch ya later, see you. (*Beat.*) Eh – yeah.

NAJMA. Is that it?

ZAC. Ah wait. (*Pause.*) Take this.

NAJMA. A horse mask?

ZAC. Yeah, yeah. I was gonna sort of – Well, cos you never, you might – might need it for something. / Like Halloween.

NAJMA. Ahuh.

Ahuh. (*Pause.*) Anyway, I put make-up on today, so I thought I won't cry. That it'll stop me but I think I'm gonna end up with panda eyes (*Beat.*) and, and smudged.

ZAC. Err I'm off to uni.

NAJMA. Woohoo!

ZAC. Yeah off to uni – (*Shouts.*) Off to uni! Yeah, it'll be fun. Yeah maybe it's not the most exciting Saturday morning we've ever had.

NAJMA. He's really sad about leaving his mummy.

ZAC. Yes, oh I don't want there to be any illusion that I am ready, I'm not at all. Chapter two Zac's life – wait or maybe three?

NAJMA. I'm gonna miss him so much. He's just so lovely and he's great company (*Beat.*) and I'm gonna miss him.

ZAC. I'm ready.

2.4.35. The future ensemble

A gauze is pulled across the stage, on to which sketches of each of the youngsters' hopes and aspirations are projected. A faint soundscape builds gently in the background underneath the dialogue.

IERUM. I had this dream once that I was born into Victorian times. Yeah. So like everyone was wearing these nice dresses and they were walking round London. Yeah, I was wearing uhm, the dress too and it was, there were like lots of green areas, like really big buildings – like little cute houses and girls playing hopscotch and it was really nice. I wish I was born in that generation.

ROBYN. I was like, 'oh I wonder what I wanna do when I grow up?' and I was like, 'let's become a forensic psychologist', and I was like, 'no let's do like blahdy, blahhh, blah-blahhh, blah-blahhh', and I was like, 'you've been writing since you were a kid just fucking do some screenwriting'. It makes me really happy.

MIA. I'm gonna carry on working, I've got a savings account, I'm gonna buy a house, I'm gonna do it up and I'm going to rent it out. An' that's gonna pay for itself and then I'm gonna carry on saving.

ZAC. I feel like most people who do a degree in Music are gonna end up in teaching so I mean the boring answer would be, I'm gonna be a teacher. I mean it sounds more interesting to say rockstar, there you go I'll be a rockstar.

CALLUM. I would like to teach but not, not lower you know I'd like to do it in a university or something as a professor. I don't think I could deal with the children to be honest; I can't, I can't stand them. Even secondary school is pushing it.

ALI. I've changed my mind you know about my career.

AYESHA. For about the hundredth thousand millionth time.

ALI. If I-I don't get my proper top grades I'm just gonna go into policing. I feel like I'm good at investigating like when something goes on at home. I'm very good at solving the crime.

AYESHA. Have you told them I call you a pig?

Laughter.

TAYLOR. Hopefully go to the Olym–, Paralympics in Tokyo.
And if I – manage to get the gold there I'll be set forever
yeah money-wise-an'. Yeah for just – throwing a ball.

AYESHA. I wanna use my young time as being naughty coz
that's the only time I'm gonna get to be. You know Primark
an' stuff? I really wanna work in Primark, I dunno why, I
have an' obsession with Primark.

EMILY. No idea what I'm doing. Hah. I want to do Life Science
at York, basically that's the only course I like in the country,
so I want to go there and do that.

LUCAS. Well I'm taking a gap year; I'm taking a camper van
through Europe, down Italy, back out of Germany, do a bit of
Spain, France, so I think that'll be pretty perfect. I just need
to learn how to drive.

LUAN. I think next year if everything goes to plan then I might
like have like my best season next year a hundred per cent.
I definitely feel like I – could'ha'like a really good season
next year. What I'm hoping.

ANNABELLA. I don't like to think about the future, like ever.
I literally haven't even thought about what I'm gonna eat for
dinner. I just think like, like I'm happy now, you know I'm
fifteen like I'm so young, I don't want to think about the
future, I want to be hap– happy like now. There's going to be
so many surprises in life, there's jus' no point in thinking
about it. I wanna get this year over at school and then (*Beat.*)
we'll see what happens then.

ANNABELLA *pulls away the gauze as a vicious sound rips
through the auditorium. The youngsters are revealed all
stood in a line wearing face masks, staring blankly at the
audience.*

Blackout.

Second interval.

PART THREE

ACT FIVE

All the interviews in this scene were carried out over the phone due to the lockdown measures. Unless otherwise specified, the interviews took place at home.

The stage remains empty until 3.5.8. The actors appear filmed, as if speaking on a live video call, projected on to the back wall.

3.5.1. A twist in the plot

JEN. Hello. (*Laughs.*) Different world isn't it from when we last met. Change to the plot, a twist in the plot.

JEN *enters* EMILY*'s bedroom.*

Yep I shall er pass you over. (*Beat.*) Oh dear she's crying, she doesn't want to talk to you / sorry okay I'm leaving her room she's umm / oh she doesn't want to talk anybody at the moment so I don't know what's up with her.

EMILY. There's no point.

I don't want to talk to you!

JEN. Yes, not in a good mood at all. Oh dear. (*Beat.*) Oh dear funny old world isn't it now.

3.5.2. I don't have corona

IERUM (*coughs*). Oh, oh, no I don't have corona do – do not worry, I definitely do not have corona. I wash my hands every day.

3.5.3. Sainsbury's own-brand vodka

ROBYN *leaves home for work.*

MIG. Wash your hands.

ROBYN. I know I've got it with me, my hand sanitiser, it's in my pocket. First we had home-made hand sanitiser, er it's like hand gel like with like, and it didn't have any alcohol in it so my parents went out and bought Sainsbury's own-brand vodka and put it in my hand gel. That's cos there's no hand gel anywhere.

3.5.4. Literally tiny

IERUM. I'd rather learn at school because umm, / (*Beat.*) b'coz there's a lot of us in the house, there's – six of us. That's pretty a lot and my house is literally tiny. The boys attack each other like every five seconds. I think coz like when we're at school we're like separate and like we have more space.

MASARRAT. Oi! Mummy's doing these.

MASOOD. Aiee!

3.5.5. Korean supermarket

ROBYN *walks along a street.*

ROBYN. Er I work in a Korean supermarket so I'm not in direct contact with the customers, so I'm in the kitchen bit. Coz it's Scotland people are just like, 'ach we'll be fine we've survived worst'. There's a part of me that's enjoying it. I feel really bad for saying it but it's true, just I'm like ohhh.

I am slightly worried about not seeing Rob yes, but (*Beat.*) I think we'll be okay, you know. It was my birthday yesterday so I'm still taking that in, like I'm that year older. What a day to turn nineteen, the place has stopped, over-seventies are not leaving the house and Tescos out of bloody pasta.

3.5.6. Three nights in Paris

LUCAS. Georgie got me the most amazing eighteenth birthday present. She'd got me three nights in Paris, but we can't go – cos of the – which is SO frustrating. School's just – all with the whole COVID-19 thing everything's kind of just – all our year group are just freaking out about what the hell exams are gonna be like. The school has spent a fortune on a new tech thing just in case we have to do our lessons online.

3.5.7. Bald head on the screen

TAYLOR. So I'm FaceTiming ma tutors to do work. I just can't wait to see my tutor's bald head on the screen. (*Laughs.*) And as well I broke my Xbox, so I have nothing to do so I'm just stuck. Like what a time yeah to break my Xbox. I don't want it to affect my training yeah, but then like I was supposed to have an exam (*Beat.*) Tuesday (*Beat.*) but I think that's been cancelled. Eer quite happy weird though coz I haven't revised for it. Coronavirus has saved Taylor and fucked up the whole world and saved me.

3.5.8. Distracted

Sitting in the car.

AYESHA. They've given me an online school website thing that I have to start at nine o'clock in the morning which um I don't have time for that, I'd be sleeping at that time. At nine o'clock in the morning I'm not gonna get ready just to look good on FaceTime-thing so. Yeah I've been told off so many times. They email my mum every morning and they even, even emailed me but I haven't opened the message yet.

ALI. I can't work at home coz there's so many people so you just get distracted really easily.

AYESHA. An' then like –

ALI. – The new baby in the house. We have to be there to help our mum out.

AYESHA. That's it.

/ ALI *coughs.*

I'm looking so nice.

Have you got corona get the fuck out ma car!

AYESHA *kicks* ALI *out of the car and the action of the play moves from the filmed video projections on the back wall to live action with the actors onstage.*

ALI *and* AYESHA *pop up in hatch, upstage-left.*

ALI. Shut up and I'll give it to you so you can die. I'll go to Wuhan and eat a bat myself just to give it to you!

AYESHA *laughs.*

Corona bona. I hate corona so bad.

3.5.9. Zombie apocalypse

The children's home.

ANNABELLA. At least it's like a virus and people are either recovering from it or dying, instead of like, I don't know like turning into zombies. Coz like zombies, zombies are terrifying, like I think people are overreacting. You know it's not like a zombie apocalypse. Like if there was a zombie apocalypse then I would be panic-buying.

3.5.10. Nice little sesh

Aunt Amanda's home.

MIA. Have you stockpiled on toilet roll? The carpet shops are doing really well, we've having one of their busiest weeks of the year this week. I think its becoz people know they're gonna be stuck in the house yeah. Amanda's yard big enough, we've got like loads to do, we're gonna clean the hot tub and stuff out so it's not like we're going to be bored. My plan is to (*Beat.*) have a nice two-week little session, a nice little sesh, couple of bottles of Prosecco, couple of cans of gin, jump in the hot tub and just relax. I've worked hard enough (*Beat.*) it's a two-week holiday.

3.5.11. Chopin's Nocturnes

JAZ*'s flat*.

ZAC. I've got a bunch of essays to do, I, look, look I find it very
hard to like get invested in, like the essays and stuff anyway.
So when it's like all this stuff happening and I'm having to
write about, you know, the use of pedal in Chopin's
Nocturnes. S'like what f'? Li'I'm sit-in there goin', 'What's
this, what's the point of this?' Like I've got 'em, I've got three
er eh, escalation points for attendance because my attendance
is so bad. (*Beat*.) Ah one of my friends umm I'm in her flat
just now. Ah she's going, she's going back to Singapore. Umm
but then like doesn't know if she'll get let back in.

3.5.12. Immune-system suppressant

CALLUM. So I went on the er these cyclosporin tablets er last
night I started them. I'm definitely a bit clearer, I'm not as
red, it's not as roaring red. It's starting to, to work I think
hopefully. It's, it's like a-a immune-system suppressant.

MARGARET. We're hopeful, we're hopefully coz we need
something to work. An' if he can get some temporary relief.
The way things are going now with the COVID-19 and we
don't know whether he'll be back at school and even if he
did get in – it's a good idea that he's around so many people.
Obviously his immune, immune system will be suppressed
and that would be (*Beat*.) you know more difficult for him to
fight off infection.

CALLUM. Need to be careful.

3.5.13. Good good friend

Same as 3.5.11.

JAZ *sits upstage on her laptop, wearing earphones*.

ZAC. My friend Jaz here she, she's like, tsh – yeah she's-just
sitting over there on her laptop. Jaz is my good, good friend.
Good friend. Not girl–, I never said the word girlfriend.

JAZ *laughs*.

What's a better word?

Pause.

JAZ. Good friend. (*Laughs*.)

ZAC. Good friend. Umm. (*Beat*.) Haha. (*Beat. Coughs*.)
I haven't even told my parents about this.

3.5.14. I can battle the virus

LULJETA. No I'm not okay, no Luan or Drin but they don't
listen – / don't understand.

DRIN. Have you, have you not seen the statistic?

LULJETA. What do you mean?

DRIN. Well how many, how many cases in the UK?

Beat.

AGRON. Five thousand.

DRIN. And then how many, what's the population of London?
(*Beat*.) Eight million.

LULJETA. Don't / be so stupid!

LUAN *laughs*.

DRIN. So what's the percentage?

LULJETA. You have to be careful.

DRIN. Well if you know – if you talk about the statistics in
this –

LULJETA. Yeah, people like you –

DRIN. – People are just getting scared for no reason.

LULJETA. AHHH!

AGRON. Are you serious / man?

LULJETA. Ohhhh man.

AGRON. / Are you serious man?

LUAN. Are you serious?

DRIN *goes to leave the room.*

AGRON. You're not going out.

LUAN. Drin, this is what I'm / thinking yeah.

DRIN. I'm safe, I'm young! / I can battle the virus. / The virus should be scared of catching me!

LUAN. Drin.

When I see Drin –

Ha. Me I'll be fine.

DRIN. It's not that deep man it's coronavirus it's not that deep. Everyone's getting worried for no reason. Give it, give it like, give it like another month and it'll all be forgotten.

3.5.15. Heavy metal

Same as 3.5.11. and 3.5.13.

ZAC. Those headphones are really noise-cancelling as well, so I know I'm safe. Wait, Jaz. Can you hear me? Can you turn the music up? (*Laughs.*)

JAZ. Yeah.

ZAC (*laughs*). Heavy metal?

JAZ. Yes.

ZAC. Alright. We won't see each other for a minimum, coz we don't know when uni's starting, a minimum of five months, it kinda sucks (*Beat.*) but just gonna roll with the punches. (*Laughs*). Five months is so long though. Fuck.

3.5.16. Rebellion

Same as 3.5.14

DRIN. I'd rather everyone just catch it now and we can get it over and done with.

LUAN. We gonna start a rebel– rebellion.

LULJETA. That's why we need the military and everybody to stop stupid people like you.

AGRON. There's your / dictator, there's your dictator.

LUAN. Huh.

DRIN. No but I sense –

AGRON. Get the army.

LULJETA. Yeah.

LUAN. The young generation we've already, we've already made a / Snapchat thing about it.

DRIN. I've had enough of all the old people running the country, it's our turn, / our turn now – (*Laughs.*)

LUAN. It's our turn!

  Yeah we've already started a rebellion and we're gonna start, the younger generation gonna start sweeping the streets up.

DRIN. When was the last time you left your house? Idris Elba has it. / Come on, everyone's got it. (*Beat.*) CORONAVIRUS! It's corona time.

  LUAN *laughs*.

LUAN. That's just a – our generation.

DRIN. What, do you think the old people think about us when they're voting in their elections?

LUAN. Ohhhhhhhhh! Yes Drin.

DRIN. Suddenly we're meant to look after them but they don't look after us.

  DRIN *puts on a jacket*.

AGRON. Goin', he look he's going out.

DRIN. I've just put some clothes on. Jesus Christ!

3.5.17. Que sera sera

Same as 3.5.11, 3.5.13 and 3.5.15.

ZAC. Que sera sera. What will be, will be. (*Beat.*) Basically, like, like, the whole like uni stuff like the – you know, the – the essays and the exams, like it's so insignificant when you think – like – like families are potentially getting split up and separated because they can't fly across.

JAZ. Well we have coursework due still. We have an essay due Friday, he's got one due-what four hours ago?

ZAC. Four, yeah.

JAZ laughs.

3.5.18. Distance social distancing

Same as 3.5.14 and 3.5.16.

LUAN *puts on his sweatshirt.*

AGRON. Luan what you doing?

LUAN. We're goin' to the park I'll be like five minutes.

AGRON. I'm not going, you don't going to the park are you?

LUAN. I'm waiting / for you lot.

AGRON. Don't be silly man.

LUAN. Why a park?

AGRON. Distance, / social distancing.

LUAN. Why can't – (*Beat.*) why can't you go for a run.

Pause.

AGRON. Oh. (*Beat.*) What an idiot.

LUAN. I'll be five minutes, you lot.

3.5.19. Fear ensemble

A threatening soundscape plays under the dialogue.

LUAN. Yeah I don't really care about getting it but (*Beat.*) nothing will happen to me most likely.

IERUM. I'm definitely, I'm not going to catch the coronavirus because I am ready. I have my hand sanitiser.

ANNABELLA. I've got like antibacterial wipes that I've been wiping my door handle with, like even my shoes and my e-cig an' my phone.

IERUM. I have lots of soap in the house, I'm-I'm like very very serious about this.

ROBYN. I'm not really panicking, I'm just being precautious.

ZAC. Umm yeah, I think I am anxious.

TAYLOR. And as well my wheelchair I'm basically fucked coz my hands are always on the floor yeah. I'm always having to wash an', be cautious yeah.

EMILY. And that doesn't really affect me if I catch it. Because I will most likely be fine.

ANNABELLA. Oh I think I'm just going to lock myself away in my room.

CALLUM. It's-it's not all bad. There's people out there who have it and they've recovered from it you know.

ALI. All the Asian people, they can fight anything.

AYESHA. Drugs, / the drugs like, everyone's like-apparently the cure is cocaine.

ALI. Yeah, everyone's like – yeah.

LUAN. I've literally done (*Beat.*) pretty much everything I could to get it.

MIA. I do wanna be responsible like but I don't, how far is it gonna go yeah, when's it gonna stop?

ANNABELLA. Is this what the world's gonna be like all summer?

LUCAS. Hell Jesus. Arrr it's jus' just, so confusing.

ANNABELLA. Whe– when does it end?

3.5.20. Terrible cough

IERUM. Basically, my dad came back with a terrible cough.
Coz he's like literally the only one who goes out. Er I'm
just thinking that (*Beat.*) maybe it's just like a normal cough
I guess. Well that's what everyone basically thinking in the
house because nobody really wants to accept the fact that it
could be coronavirus. And I'm just umm (*Beat.*) worried
and stuff.

3.5.21. Bit of a flu

LUCAS. Dad's, Dad's ill at the moment and we think he might
have it. He's fine though, he's fine, it's-it, he just, he just in
bed with a bit of a flu er and a, and a temperature. He's in a,
he's in one of the (*Beat.*) spare rooms. He's still working,
he's got his laptop and he's on calls constantly.

3.5.22. Laying down in her bed

IERUM. My mum she isn't really feeling well today umm she
says it's just a cough but I'm thinking maybe otherwise.
But she was like coughing bad like this morning she was like
laying down (*Beat.*) in-o-in her bed. I'm thinking that she
may have caught it from my dad. An' I – I – I really don't
want to catch it.

3.5.23. Exams are off

LUCAS. Exams are off – va– which is sh-shite (*Laughs.*) I
mean I never thought I'd ever say that, but (*He lights his
cigarette.*) I wish exams were on. Ah my mood has been
fluctuating massively because you hear there's no exams and
you're like, 'ah sweet' and then you're like, 'ah'. I mean
actually I kind of wanted to do them. I've worked so bloody

hard, look I mean the smallest, the small thing of you know,
'fuck me the exams are over, yeah!' I was quite looking
forward to it and now I kinda feel lost, umm.

3.5.24. Paranoid

IERUM. There's a thing I read the other day about this twenty-
one-year-old woman she, she doesn't have, she doesn't have
asthma her parents confirmed that she didn't have any health
issues or health problems and she died from the coronavirus.
It really got me bad.

3.5.25. Heart close up

ZAC. Jaz's gone umm she left on Sunday ahhhhhh and yeah.
I went to the airport with her. Er yeah it was, it was, it was
pretty sad. It was quite funny ah like after s'like she'd kind of
walked away (*Laughs.*) say goodbye, I turned around and I
was like my instinct – I just really wanted to hit something. So
I just like smacked the side of my thigh as hard as I could, but
it made like a really big like 'smack' sound. (*Laughs.*) I just
literally felt my heart go like ffft just close up. (*Laughs.*) It
was – which was really odd. I didn't expect it to be that like
like umm not-not physical but like – an' I was like, 'ah I'm
empty inside'. No but it, it def, it definitely is love.

3.5.26. Bleach

TAYLOR. Bad day today. (*Beat.*) Stressed. My dad's, basically,
in the nicest way my dad's a-a (*Beat.*) shithead. (*Beat.*) We
h've – hah-we have this spray when we go in and out of the
house we have to spray ourselves down, and the dumbass
has only gone and changed the spray with bleach okay?
Didn't tell me and I've just sprayed myself with bleach.
(*Beat.*) I've had like stained, like stinging eyes for like the
past twenty minutes. Just not my day today. And umm not
done much college work. I'd rather chill. (*Beat.*) It's fun
though, I don't mind being off. One good thing about ley-
like about my mum being a hairdresser yeah, everyone looks

like, like proper rough yeah and we just got fresh cuts the whole time.

KEG *get up from his chair.*

Keg's moving. First time today he's moved – (*Laughs*.) Yeah the WiFi really is shit at home.

KEG. Hard life being an eighteen-year-old in quarantine.

TAYLOR. Yeah.

KEG. When your WiFi's broke.

3.5.27. Stabby

ROBYN *and* MIG *are watching the news, the volume is down.*

MIG. Yer man's on the telly now.

ROBYN. Ahhhhh.

MIG. There he is. Mind you he doesn't look so happy to be prime minister now. / That Rishi Ssssunak.

ROBYN (*laughs*). He's just out of school. He's twelve.

MIG. Thatcher would have done a better job. (*Beat*.) De– you're kinda going and I hate Thatcher. We're much happier with Nicola Sturgeon up here. (*Beat*.) It's bringing out the absolute worst in me. I feel stabby. Whenever I'm in a supermarket. (*Beat*.) I'm actually hating everyone, who's stockpiled. You, you –

ROBYN. We have stockpiled!

MIG. We stockpiled for Brexit not / for this!

ROBYN. I know. I'm not accusing.

MIG. You are accusing.

ROBYN. No, no you're paranoid.

MIG. No no. You do. Just like to stir it up that way you really do. / We're gonna kill one another if we're left in this / house for months.

ROBYN. It's not.

We are, because she's – mental.

MIG. Because she such a stirrer.

ROBYN. I'm not a stirrer. My god I am gonna kill you.

MIG. No I'm gonna kill you first.

3.5.28. Separate

ZAC. My parents, they actually decided to separate in
November, yeah (*Beat*.) yeah. I was just kinda like, 'oh that
sucks'. Ah, yeah, errrugh. That's that. The worst, the worst
possible time to – in that sort of relationship – to have a
lockdown when you can't leave. I mean it's their fucking
fault for getting married in the first place, do you know what
I mean? (*Laughing*.) You know. It wasn't my idea, they
didn't consult me or my sister about it. Oh there's Jaz, so
that's fine. That's the, that's the one thing, it's one er positive
thing that I can, I can keep going. She has flights booked for
June.

3.5.29. Spoilt bitch

Same as 3.5.26.

KEG. No I don't think he's been missing Leena to be fair. He's
j', he's been moody though so maybe I don't know yeah.

TAYLOR. I'm not, I just sprayed myself with fucking bleach
you dumbarse! (*Laughs*.) So we just message each other,
other than that it's alright. And I phone her every night.
Every night for four years. (*Laughs*.)

DYLAN. Fuckin' hell she whinges over me. Jesus Christ man!

TAYLOR. An' every time I'm in my house obviously Dylan's
with me yeah and then he comes on to the FaceTime call or
something and she's like, 'oh can't it just be like me and you,
me and you?' Yeah and I'm on Xbox with him and I'm with
him in the day yeah, she was just a bit annoyed.

DYLAN. Spoilt bitch… Tell your stupid girlfriend to calm
down. I'm your brother from another mother and I wanna
play Xbox with you alright.

3.5.30. Just as boring

MIA. Now I'm living in my boyfriend's house with his mum,
his little sister, his dad and her, my, his little sister's
boyfriend so – there's (*Beat.*) six of us, I left Amandera's
house because I just got bored and I thought I was clever.
Don't get me wrong I love it up here but wow it's (*Beat.*) just
as boring.

3.5.31. Four thousand nine hundred people died

AGRON. We're all bored – (*Sighs.*) Very scary, it's four
thousand nine hundred people died. (*Beat.*) It's not good.
I think it's serious you know. But, funny enough it's so many
people outside today you know. It beggars belief. (*Beat.*)
There's plenty of people, there's like there's nothing you
know (*Beat.*) happening. Crazy!

LUAN. I've been exercising a bit, doing what I need to do, to
stay in shape. I just want everything to start up again coz I'm
getting bored.

AGRON. I think it's, it's nearing the, the, the top of the peak
isn't it.

    LULJETA *enters with vitamins and a glass of water.*

    We take about five or six sorts of vitamins you know –
(*Laughs*). Here we go, Mum brought the vitamins for Luan.

LULJETA. Because he, he woke up today late / and he he he
runs from our ho– from our-our house to London Eye.

AGRON. / He woke up late.

LUAN. An' I run at night and it's literally, there's literally no
one. So I'm just tryna stay, stay fit really.

AGRON. I went on er Monday I think. I said, 'um just let me just go out'. Three hours nobody came in my cab, nobody. It's just so scary you know, and I love London you know it's, to see like that it pains me – it really does.

DRIN. Please stay indoors, stay safe, protect the NHS.

3.5.32. I'm so stressed

ALI. Argh, I've been getting coursework. An' like – they're giving me assignments an' I just can't do it, cos we're bored at home so they're giving us extra work to do which is making us even more boring / bored.

AYESHA. Exactly.

ALI. How do you expect us to be helping with our families. Look okay, we're with our families, half of our families are at home, we need to help our families here! You're giving us work on top of that? You should pause it for a little bit! Ya know what I mean? I'm so stressed an' you're throwing me – er – assignments from each direction. I've been emailing Ofqual telling them that I will file a complaint against this rule that they're making because I don't feel as if I'm being valued, towards my right as a British citizen.

AYESHA *laughs*.

It's not funny, I don't know why you're laughing?! (*Beat.*) Wait, sorry give me one second. The baby's crying, I'm telling you.

AYESHA. Well look bring the baby here to me. (*Beat.*) Pick her up.

ALI. The baby's crying, go and get her!

3.5.33. Sleep ensemble

The youngsters lie on the floor in darkness, just lit by the
screens on their phones, as they scroll.

IERUM. I just, I didn't have enough sleep last night, s– I'm
   really really tired coz I slept at four coz I was washing my
   hair.

ALI. I've been like sleeping at like at six in the morning and
   waking up at like four.

EMILY. I value my sleep. I still wake up at like nine.

IERUM. If that's okay – if – if you do it another day. (*Yawns.*)
   Sorry.

LUCAS. Waking up late, going to bed late.

ZAC. You sleep from you know (*Beat.*) eight in the morning till
   eight in the evening.

CALLUM. Like last night it was 'bout half-three, the last time
   I checked the clock.

EMILY. Nope. Still be going to bed at ten.

AYESHA. Mine's like, going to bed at like yeah – six and then
   wake up at two.

TAYLOR. I don't sleep till like three now and then I just wake
   up at like ten.

MIA. I go to sleep at like two, three in the morning and then
   I wake up at like three in the afternoon.

LUCAS. I'll have breakfast at three in the afternoon.

ROBYN. I feel like going to sleep at four and waking up at
   twelve.

TAYLOR. I put my TV on, so there's background noise and
   then just watch TikToks until like three in the morning.

MIA. And then I'm having a drink, and then I'm going to sleep.
   Same trip different day.

ALI. You just get bored, like I'm even getting bored of sleeping
   now.

TAYLOR. I don't even know what day it is any more you know.

ROBYN. I don't have a body clock; I don't have a body clock.

ZAC. Sometimes you just miss daylight completely – and then
you wake up and then (*Beat*.) all the sun's gone.

If you don't have anything to wake up for then (*Beat*.) you
know there's less incentive to actually (*Beat*.) you know,
wake up.

CALLUM. Yeah, there's no schedule.

ZAC. Yeah there's no structure, that's, that's it. An' if there's no
structure then, you know, y' find yourself just falling apart.

ROBYN. None of us have any reason to go to sleep. I feel like
I'm going mad.

ANNABELLA. I'm still in bed.

AGRON. Let me just call Luan. Luan can you come? He's
asleep. I can't believe it. Ah it's half-past one. This is the
currant-tine time.

3.5.34. Aloe vera plant

IERUM. I have news. Two days ago (*Beat*.) – umm (*Beat*.)
I came to a decision that I was going to get myself a s– an'
aloe vera plant. We don't really have like alive um plants
(*Beat*.) in my house. So having a – plant I think would really
like, change things for the better. Something alive – (*Beat*.)
is actually coming to my house and it's living there. It's not
just a plant, it's like a, like – (*Beat*.) like another life. I-I –
I was just pretty excited about it.

3.5.35. Garden

LUCAS. And I am so lucky that I am (*Beat*.) in a position
where I have a garden. Um I mean little things like I can
come out for a cigarette. But people who are living in the
city or living in apartments – (*Beat*.) Jesus.

3.5.36. Name

Same as 3.5.34.

IERUM. I was wondering on giving it a name, but (*Beat.*) I
don't know. I'm – I'm not sure what kind of name to give-
th'it. I've thought of umm (*Beat.*) ahh plant.

3.5.37. Gym room

LUCAS. On the other side of our house we have a (*Beat.*) very
(*Beat.*) small (*Beat.*) gym room with a bunch of equipment
ah so I've just been on the cross trainer.

3.5.38. Symptoms all gone

IERUM. The symptoms from my parents are-all gone a few
days afterwards. I might have overreacted a bit.

IERUM*'s mother is heard ticking off her siblings in the
background.*

Oh my god, wait. I'm, I'm so sorry for like the noise.

Arghh, my brother never listens. I definitely think that
(*Beat.*) I should be going back to school.

3.5.39. Made a will

MARGARET. Well um I'm still working as you know in the
hospital. You're just seeing more and more and more coming
in, the last couple of days has been a massive increase. We
had a wee boy that looked about seven or eight, we've had a
baby in.

CALLUM. You know, there's been-there's been ss– you know
work sent home and you can kinda do it online and submit it
but I mean there's – there's nowhere near enough – er – work
there to actually keep you occupied for the week.

RONALD. For some reason I had never made a will, I'm sure
they're millions of people like trying to make wills sort of,

I've actually drafted one, I got a template. You need two
people to witness it. (*Beat*.) I'm gonna have to stop the
binmen.

3.5.40. I miss my mum

ANNABELLA. Well, I'm working really hard on like fixing my
relationship with my mum. I went down and it was actually
really nice to-spend time with her. I'm really hopin' that –
you know, I'll be able to go back (*Beat*.) and live with her.
Being like in lockdown has actually made me realise how
much I miss my mum.

3.5.41. Bit of a breakdown

MIA. I'm in my dad's caravan in Nefyn. It's turned out for the
best, we're both enjoyin' it. Coming to my dad wa– was the
best thing for me mentally because, it's out the way and just
on the road to the beach and like I got time to build myself
back up. In the beginning of lockdown I had like a bit of a
breakdown and the doctors put me on antidepressants and I
just – stopped taking them and I'm kinda like fine again now.

3.5.42. Psychiatrist dude

On the street, smoking.

LUCAS. Well I'm, I'm in Saffron Walden at the moment. Umm
(*Beat*.) just (*Beat*.) I have to just wait to see my psychiatrist
dude umm (*Beat*.) but yeah I started seeing a psychiatrist.
And – I've been seeing him for a – for a bit. I never know,
I never know when to really bring it up – (*Laughs*). I had a,
I had a complete (*Beat*.) breakdown. Eh – an' it kind of all
started after GCSEs and with all the stress of that and I think
it was just a, a reserve er feelings from me that I was you
know doing less than my brothers. And I think I got, I got
tired of always putting on a – happy face – when sometimes
I wasn't. I got really pissed off at myself for being, feeling
down. Cos I was like, 'oh why?' you know, 'why should I

feel down?' I live in a (*Beat*.) gorgeous house, I go to a great school – Best thing I've ever done er opening up and saying that I need to see someone. I think most people – (*Beat*.) ha-have, have issues at this time and I know that umm you know – puberty and teenage years a – shit show really for most people, so (*Beat*.) I'm just kinda, w-waiting on this to, this to pass.

3.5.43. Here to suffer

ROBYN. What is it all for? What is it all for? We're just here to suffer. Haaa. If Boris Johnson is not dead by the end of this, I'm gonna go down Westminster an' finish the job.

3.5.44. Shaved my head

AYESHA. You know what I need – I need to have a one-o-one call with Boris Johnson.

ALI. So it'd be us three den.

AYESHA. I would scream at him. I would make him feel so low about himself. Serve him right. An' you's a fat shit yeah. / Get your country (*Laughs*.) get the country back together, because you know you're starting to piss me off.

   ALI *laughs*.

ALI. I've shaved my head.

   Laughter.

AYESHA. Yeah, man looks like Megamind.

ALI. Shut up. I took a selfie of myself but then I deleted it.

AYESHA. Yeah coz your forehead was looking so big.

ALI. Go and get your beard waxed.

AYESHA. I've been jumping on TikTok too much.

ALI. Yeah TikToking.

   A TikTok video of ALI *and* AYESHA *is projected onto the back wall.*

AYESHA. Ya know what it is? I've been watching them and then they're do you know wh–, it makes – the girls are so like, the people are so pretty they make me insecure, so late at night. At like five o' clock I'll be doing my make-up. It's so sad! Because my eyebrows are grown out! Fuckin' quarantine!

ALI *laughs*.

I'd be looking so butters and these girls be put-loading videos looking like fuckin' / shnacks.

ALI. Shnacks.

3.5.45. Massive poll

LUCAS. Elland are one of the only schools that are doing these assessments. A massive poll was started, and it got five hundred signatures. Coz we all felt so guilty coz all our mates in other schools have no chance – to boost their grades. The only up it's so (*Beat.*) glad of my friends because it is the first time they've truly gone, 'you know what Lucas, we just feel like overprivileged piece of shit'. (*Beat.*) Dad's fully recovered which is nice.

3.5.46. Chillax

EMILY. It's a bit more chillax now, like you can go see like groups like six or so people and (*Beat.*) like there's – the Cam River's quite big so there's loads of places in Elland where you can go and sit back down by. And then I've been tutoring (*Beat.*) er today and yesterday. It's a boy in the year beneath me at school. His dad's paying me, so I'm gonna buy myself some new shoes.

3.5.47. Chinese delivery

TAYLOR*'s car.*

TAYLOR. I'm sitting outside the local Chinese with Keg, been asked to help and I'm just (*Beat.*) getting out the house by driving him everywhere.

KEG. No, we do get paid. Ya get a free meal at the end of the night, so that's always a bonus.

TAYLOR. No, listen – every fucking time yeah, I'a – I say, 'oh Keg can I have fried chicken chow mein please?' Keg asked for chicken fried rice. / Okay. Every time.

KEG *laughs.*

3.5.48. Broken up

ROBYN. I-well – I got – another job because the work at the food stall closed (*Beat.*) and we can't afford me not to be working. I've got bills to pay now and I was like eut, and I pay my mum a hundred pounds every month anyway so. (*Beat.*) Me and Rob have broken up. (*Laughs*). It just wasn't working out through lockdown, just wasn't feeling it any more. It's not my first love that's like far too romantic, god no!

3.5.49. Chicken balls

Same as 3.5.47.

TAYLOR. What did you get I didn't know what you got?

KEG. Chicken balls. (*Laughs.*)

TAYLOR. You see what did I say right – Keg has got me fuck-all from the Chinese – (*Laughs.*) Every time. (*Pause.*)

Jesus!

3.5.50. Picking asparagus

LUCAS. I'm starting a job tomorrow. I'm picking asparagus. It's at, it's at India's dad's farm. (*Beat.*) And I was just over ah – at a mate's playing tennis coz they said you can play sports against one other, so... It was good, I haven't played tennis in ages ah apart, apart from on our makeshift tennis court, in the garden. It's great, I mean the bounce is a bit dodge (*Beat.*) ah (*Beat.*) but it's a good laugh. It's really not that bad here. Um. I'm very fortunate.

3.5.51. Burgers for dinner

LUCAS. All into Edinburgh. Oh, a bloody relief.

EMILY. I got into York so I'm very happy. But yeah, so it's all good. Mum's cooking burgers for dinner which I'm excited about. (*Beat.*) I bought, I bought those shoes that I wanted, I love them, they're amazing.

LUAN. Coz COVID's kind of ruined the Euros this summer so I've – I've decided to further my education and go Bournemouth University. So, they've also got basketball professional team called South Coast Tigers. Eh, they've just literally, they literally given me the thumbs-up regardless what I get I can – go. I'm gonna go.

TAYLOR. 'Hi Taylor (*Beat.*) at last your results have been certified by BTEC. Congratulations you have now passed the course with a final grade of a pass. See you on Tuesday.'

3.5.52. Shops are opening

AYESHA*'s phone rings.*

AYESHA. Oh shit that's my school calling. (*She rejects the call.*)

ALI. A lot of things are getting back to normal slowly, like-the shops are opening and ah I've just been out an' about I'm applying for jobs. It's not-it's just the fact that I wanna get out of my house, I want to do something, because there's not

– not that much to do right now. (*Beat*.) Eh, yeah, we-the shops are opened on Monday fifteenth and then we went on time at nine o'clock in the morning on that day.

AYESHA. Yeah.

ALI (*laughs*). That's how thingy we were.

3.5.53. Mia, I love you

MIA. I'm living in a trailer with, in Nefyn. Umm, I've got a boyfriend call– I've got a new boyfriend called Cai and we're both really happy together. We've got a dog. What is she babe?

CAI. She's a Labrador.

MIA. She's a Labrador crossed with a sheep dog. Ah say hi babe –

CAI. Hi ya, you're alright?

MIA. Introduce yourself like, 'Hi I'm Cai.'

CAI. Hi ya I'm Cai. Umm Cai Morgan-Jones –

MIA. – No you're Mia's boyfriend.

CAI. Oh, I'm Mia's boyfriend yeah.

MIA. I have sorted myself out this time. I've said it a few times yeah but this time I mean it.

CAI. Yeah we're happy yeah. She's the best thing that's ever happened to me to be honest with ya.

MIA. Awwww. (*Beat*.) I wasn't expecting that. (*Chuckles*.)

CAI. I do love her. I do love her. A lot.

MIA. Yeah, he tells me he loves me real – It was last night, I was sat there watching a film, when we went to sleep, he was like, 'I love you, love you. Mia, I love you'. I am really happy, everything going really well at the minute yeah. (*Beat*.) An' it can only go up now yeah.

3.5.54. His girlfriend

ALI. I'm going out next week as well with my friend.

AYESHA. His girlfriend.

ALI. Ayesha! Well basically I haven't fully been out with her like – I haven't been fully out like you knows, we're going out on Monday. You know what, when you actually get in a relationship yeah, you lit' – it's soo different to like being not in one, d'you get what I mean? You can only just focus on them and you just have to basically like reply to them all the time but – (*Beat.*) and I can't even be alone during the night to watch my phone, watch programmes, coz I just have to be on call with her. And like, I-wanna-watch-catch up on *EastEnders* but I can't even do that no more.

3.5.55. Excuses to drink

LUCAS. It's gonna be warm this week, wow. I'm actually going to see Georgie (*Beat.*) umm which'll be lovely, and she has a pool so it's kind of the perfect week. I'm trying to have (*Beat.*) a few days – without alcohol – but I'm finding it difficult (*Beat.*) but there-ahh-we, we always find excuses to drink, that's the problem. (*Laughs*) And I'm also trying to – (*Clears his throat.*) I'm-I'm I'm going, on an attempt to only smoke five cigarettes a day (*Beat.*) for a week.

3.5.56. Peace in my room

IERUM *shows off her aloe vera plant.*

IERUM. I've been taking care of my aloe vera plant; this is it right now, it's-a very happy plant, and it grew. I feel like the plants in my house are like, more of a sense of peace in my room. I mean because they don't, they're alive but they just – they don't – they w-yeah they don't talk they're just – (*Beat.*) there.

3.5.57. CBT

ROBYN. Had an appointment with a psychiatrist the other, er
yesterday. It was quite heavy but it was good. They're gonna
get me referred to CBT. It's a form of behavioural therapy
which will hopefully, hopefully help (*Beat.*) the anxiety –
(*Beat.*) and the intrusive thoughts that I don't wish to dwell
on right now coz I'm doing quite well today.

3.5.58. Thirteen years' worth of piano music

ZAC. My parents have decided to sell the house which only
makes sense. So, we've gotta, me-m– we being myself and
my sister, we've gotta move all our stuff out of, you know
(*Beat.*) our childhood home. Yesterday I went through twelve
years' worth, no sorry thirteen years' worth of-of er piano
music. Sometimes I'm like, 'oh for fuck's sake!' I am
currently in Edinburgh looking for (*Beat.*) a flat to move
into. Umm (*Beat.*) I'm staying in Jaz's, eh-Jaz's flat umm but
(*Beat.*) because I don't have a flat to move into, I don't have
a place to put all this stuff but hey ho. (*Beat.*) Keep, keep
going.

3.5.59. NHS clap ensemble

Clapping starts gently.

LULJETA. Today we're-today we lost, we lost er one of our
colleagues from COVID-19. I always go out and clap. /
They've already started.

AGRON. Oh they're starting.

ALI. This is Sparkbrook, nobody's gonna clap.

AYESHA. Honestly no one.

ALI. I think it's mostly people are concerned about Ramadan
this –

AYESHA. Yeah.

ZAC. I think it's Boogie for Boris is the official hashtag.

Clapping builds.

LUCAS. Can you hear the church bells?

Church bells toll.

Ahh! Yep I can hear pots and pans, I can hear clapping.

Clapping crescendo.

ZAC. / Yaaas! C'mon!!

LUCAS. Whoa. WHOAA!!!!!

Clapping decrescendo.

ROBYN. Ah well that was enough excitement for one day. Ah there's something to do.

ACT SIX

Interviews resumed to in-person as lockdown restrictions now lifted.

Over the course of these final scenes, as each youngster's story comes to an end, they take up a seated position, either on a chair or cross-legged on the floor in front, to create a tableau like a formal school photo.

3.6.1. Make-up on my collar

At home. ANNABELLA *wears her new school blazer.*

ALBERTA. Oh the blue blazer, that's lovely.

ANNABELLA. I hate it.

ALBERTA. I know but it's to distinguish you from the others isn't it, that you're a sixth year.

ANNABELLA *looks at herself in the mirror.*

ANNABELLA. Oh my god I have make-up on my collar already. (*Beat.*) Wait I need to see what I look like. (*Beat.*) I'm so nervous but I'm like happy that my foundation looks really nice. I literally, I did everything I could to make my face like smooth. I shaved my face, and I drank nothing but water for the past like two / three days.

ALBERTA. Why? – You never shave your face what the hell are you doing / shaving –

ANNABELLA. You always, you shave your face or it's not completely smooth and I bin like scrubbing it –

ALBERTA. You'll end up with a zit. / You'll end –

ANNABELLA. Yeah but look how-how nice it looks now. / My foundation looks so good today.

ALBERTA *laughs.*

3.6.2. Hurry up!

TASMIN (*shouting*). This girl takes hours! Your eyebrows are fine! (*Laughs.*) Come down and put your skirt on! (*Beat.*) I'm kind of stuck in a dilemma. Because if she get – she's got CPE infection –

ALI. – Uzma

TASMIN. – An' if she gets any infections – (*Beat.*) there's no cure. They all been told that they're not allowed to hug anybody, that's why we've kind of had to distance – everything.

AYESHA *runs on, near hysterical.*

AYESHA. Where's the masks? I'm so stressed. I'm going into Year 11. I've got my GCSE this year. My mum wants me to rush. I'm stressed out!

ALI. She's on a mad one.

TASMIN. Shut up and hurry up!

AYESHA. Oh chi zu school tha lorashama.

TASMIN (*yelling*). Oh get out!

AYESHA (*yelling back*). Okay I'm coming!

3.6.3. Smile

At home. CALLUM *wears his new school blazer.*

CALLUM. I finished my medication. Ah so. Yeah, yeah. I won't be at, ya know, any greater risk than, any other, hopefully.

MARGARET *hands* CALLUM *his face mask.*

MARGARET. Don't forget your mask.

He'll have to sort of get ready to head down. (*Beat.*) I'll just take his photograph.

CALLUM *smiles for the photo.*

Alright? Smile!

MARGARET *takes a photo.*

3.6.4. Big Fish

At home. Loading up the car with luggage.

LUAN. Yeah I am feeling good man, I'm excited. They've given the go ahead for October November for the BBL. So that's the professional league.

AGRON. The games are televised.

LUAN. If we make the finals as well – we'll be on the BBC.

AGRON. He's a big fish now. (*Clicking fingers.*) My guy. (*Clicking fingers.*) My guy.

3.6.5. GCSEs are not a joke

On the way to school.

AYESHA. I haven't bought a mask, oh shit, they can give me one in school, I'm not paying for a mask. We're not allowed to hug or touch. We're not allowed, and (*Pause.*) I think we're jus' gonna do it anyways. Oh my God I'm so scared. Ya-know, I used to think oh my God GCSEs are a joke; GCSEs are not a joke I just realised.

3.6.6. I don't know if I can do it

On the way to school.

IERUM. I was in Year 10 for like five minutes and then (*Beat.*) I'm suddenly in Year 11. So I missed all that like umm Year 10 stuff that I needed, that's why I'm not really happy with Corona. Now it's just like, oh my God, like I'm in Year 11 (*Beat.*) and (*Beat.*) my GCSEs are literally in a few months. (*Beat.*) Ah – I don't know if I can do it. Ah-cos-it's been like such a mess.

3.6.7. I'm not fuckin' cryin'

At home.

TAYLOR. It's a two-year course so, I'll be like (*Beat.*) a qualified coach at the end.

GEORGE. Yeah, I'm happy.

TAYLOR. Before you start crying ya know. He's bin crying for a bit.

GEORGE. I'll miss the little bastard already yeah. I'm not crying you idiot.

TAYLOR. Really yeah.

GEORGE. I'm not fuckin' cryin'!

3.6.8. We'll miss her

At home, packing for university.

JEN. An' I'm gonna miss her yeah. I know she spends a lot of time in her room and she's been out quite a bit but it's just having that, knowing somebody's there as well and you can / bump in the kitchen and you know argue over the kettle or you know.

EMILY. I literally don't spend any time in my room, what are you talking about?

JEN. Yeah, we'll we'll miss her an awful lot, erm…

EMILY. I don't spend any time in my room.

3.6.9. Getting married

On the way to college.

ALI. My last year at college now. I'm literally soo nervous. Being in a (*Beat.*) relationship – it's fun but tiring. No actually she's really really nice, I really like her. I just hope everything works out in the end. And then (*Beat.*) get married. (*Clicks his cheek.*) Like I can't believe it, like the other day I was in Year 6 and now look at me now, last year of college.

3.6.10. Smooth operator

Same as 3.6.4.

AGRON. O ricky ta ka te, o ricky ta ka ta. Let's go. Here we go, hey look, look, look.

   AGRON *takes out a smoothie machine from one of the bags.*

   (*Sings.*) Smooth operator. Smooth machine, yeah.

   Beat.

DRIN. Oh my god.

   AGRON *laughs.*

   That was such a Dad moment.

AGRON. Why you all laughing with Dad? What's so wrong?

DRIN. We're not laughing, we're laughing at you. (*Beat.*) Not with you though.

   LUAN *and* LULJETA *arrive with the last bags.*

AGRON. That's it son.

LUAN. Nah.

   DRIN *hugs* LUAN *tightly.*

DRIN. Enjoy yourself. (*Beat.*) See you soon.

   A schoolgirl walks past.

LUAN. Look at that guy, look at that. That used to be me.

LULJETA. Huh?

AGRON. I know.

DRIN. Heheh.

LULJETA. Ah – it used to be you, yeah I know.

LUAN. But I wouldn't leave this early, I'd leave about eight-ten just five minutes before school. And I'd be jogging to school like, 'ah no'. I –

LULJETA. – Hey!

LUAN. I've learnt my lessons now. I'm good, I'm good, I'm good, I'm good.

3.6.11. Gap year

At home.

LUCAS. So some of my mates they're already in lockdown in unis and – ah ju' – miserable. So I'm (*Beat.*) thankful with the gap year. Year off now, get some money (*Beat.*) do some (*Beat.*) travel.

3.6.12. Resilient

CAI*'s mum's house.*

MIA. 2020 showed me yeah – (*Beat.*) I'm stronger than I thought. My dad fucked up though, I don't be with him. I never want be with him. I'll never speak to him again. I moved up to here, Cai's mum's house. (*Beat.*) I know, it's nice though, yeah? Look at all this yeah. I ha', I'm resilient yeah. Ca', I'm lucky yeah, I've landed on my feet with Cai. His dad owns a big like mo– like a lorry firm in Gloucester. So we can both go up there, there's work there for us. He's gonna pay, he's gonna put me through my test. I just need to pass my theory. I've been smashing my theory for days upstairs yeah. I'm determined now yeah.

3.6.13. Aged

ZAC. In the past year I feel I've like aged, more than I did, haha, in the previous eighteen like, you know like the parents – (*Beat.*) getting split up and then (*Beat.*) COVID and then (*Beat.*) you know like-whe, just all the stuff happens an' I – but then the thing is, ev– everyone's had a tough year.

3.6.14. Festive bake from Greggs

ROBYN. I'm on propranolol. Um it's a beta blocker so, so if I get like a palpitation, I'll just pop one of those, just like candy. 2020 is the fucking worst year ever. I can't do this any fucking more and Sean Connery died today, after everything! See if I don't get a festive bake from Greggs I'm fucking ending it.

3.6.15. That bird off *Frozen*

MIA. I've calmed down like, I've sorted myself out, like I've calmed down loads. I've just let everything go. I'm like that bird off *Frozen*, Elsa yeah. Just let it go. I've just (*Beat.*) grown up. (*Beat.*) Euhh – did I say that? Euhh.

3.6.16. I'm growing up

ROBYN. I have felt the impact that this has had on my generation. We've been left in the rubble! There's no such thing as a new normal, it just is what it is – you know. It's just we're constantly adapting to everyday changes that are frequently impacting our lives until we're fucking, are sixty years old with arthritis and gout, climbing about an old people's home. It's like fuck I'm growing up.

3.6.17. Replacements

IERUM. So I was sitting and I was umm daydreaming a bit, then I looked around my class and like I was like, 'wow like these people I've been with for since Year 7', you know like this is our like, this is like the last couple of months that we're going be with each other. We – there's a really high possibility that none of us will ever see each other again (*Beat.*) because we'll all enter and join society and become – what (*Beat.*) people were before. Like I just saw us as (*Beat.*) replacements for those that either had passed away or either had umm stopped doing a certain job. Like is it jus' going to continue being like every year like a new set of kids being born, a new set of students entering school, a new set of students leaving, finishing their GCSEs, a new set finishing university. (*Beat.*)

The three adults enter and take up their positions as teachers, standing behind the two rows of youngsters.

Is this it now? (*Beat.*) Are you gonna end it now? No, no, no. Ohhh, umm (*Beat.*) final words.

A long pause.

Umm. (*Laughs*). Umm. Mmmm. (*Pause*.) Goodbye world.

Blackout.

The End.

www.nickhernbooks.co.uk

facebook.com/nickhernbooks

twitter.com/nickhernbooks